Norway Travel Guide

Captivating Adventures through Must-See Places, Local Culture, Norwegian Landmarks, Hidden Gems, and More

Welcome Aboard, Discover Your Limited-Time Free Bonus!

Hello, traveler! Welcome to the Captivating Travels family, and thanks for grabbing a copy of this book! Since you've chosen to join us on this journey, we'd like to offer you something special.

Check out the link below for a FREE Ultimate Travel Checklist eBook & Printable PDF to make your travel planning stress-free and enjoyable.

But that's not all - you'll also gain access to our exclusive email list with even more free e-books and insider travel tips. Well, what are you waiting for? Click the link below to join and embark on your next adventure with ease.

Access your bonus here:
https://livetolearn.lpages.co/checklist/
Or, Scan the QR code!

Table of Contents

Introduction

Do you wish to trek through untouched wilderness, gaze in awe at cascading fjords, or taste freshly caught seafood under the midnight sun? Norway is a majestic landscape of icy glaciers, vibrant coastal towns, and historic cities just waiting to be explored. But where to begin?

Forget sifting through mountains of online articles or deciphering confusing guidebooks. This Norway Travel Guide is your Viking compass, the perfect companion for crafting an unforgettable adventure, even if you've never stepped foot on Scandinavian soil. With this guide, you'll navigate bustling Oslo like a local, effortlessly hopping between museums, vibrant cafes, and the iconic Holmenkollen ski jump. You'll find glacier-carved valleys to hike in Western Norway and experience the midnight sun in Lofoten.

Norway and its regions.[1]

With the following chapters, you'll unlock the secrets to Norway without being pummeled by dense jargon and confusing maps common to other travel books. Instead, you'll have a clear, step-by-step guide for everything from getting to the airport to booking a cabin by the fjord. It'll equip you with insider tips, from hidden local gems to navigating public transportation like a pro!

We've even provided a list of basic Norwegian phrases to charm the locals, amazing itineraries (but with budget-friendly options), and a list of experiences you won't want to miss.

No prior Viking training is required. Whether you're a seasoned traveler or a wide-eyed adventurer, this guide caters to all levels. It'll introduce you to Norway's rich history, vibrant culture, and stunning landscapes, ensuring you experience its magic, not just see it. Each chapter of "Norway Travel Guide" is a portal to a new wonder:

- **Chapter 1:** Get to Know Norway: Unravel the country's soul, from Viking sagas to modern marvels.

- **Chapter 2:** To and From the Airport: Seamless transfers, like a magic carpet ride to your adventure.

- **Chapter 3:** Oslo: Norway's Capital: Explore streets where history whispers and modern art screams.

- **Chapter 4:** Eastern Norway (Østlandet): Hike through forests where trolls once roamed and discover canal towns.

- **Chapter 5:** Southern Norway (Sørlandet): Bask on golden beaches, kayak through turquoise waters, and savor fresh seafood feasts.

- **Chapter 6:** Western Norway (Vestlandet): Cruise through fjord masterpieces, witness glaciers calving into icy seas, and lose yourself in coastal villages.

- **Chapter 7:** Central Norway (Trøndelag): Dive into Viking history, explore vibrant Trondheim, and hike through breathtaking mountain landscapes.

- **Chapter 8:** Northern Norway (Nord-Norge): Chase, the Northern Lights, witness the midnight sun and experience the raw beauty of the Arctic.

- **Chapter 9:** Itineraries and Programs: Craft your perfect adventure, from weekend escapes to epic journeys.

- **Bonus Chapter:** Useful Norwegian Survival Phrases: Charm your way through bakeries, shops, and maybe even a Viking reenactment!

So, pack your sense of wonder, lace up your boots, awaken your inner Viking, and let's go embrace the breathtaking beauty of Norway!

Chapter 1: Get to Know Norway

Norway, the land of the midnight sun, towering fjords, and Viking sagas, beckons with an enchanting melody of nature's grandeur and cultural charm. Before you embark on your Nordic adventure, take some time to bask in the essence of this country, equipping yourself with the knowledge to navigate its depths and unlock its secrets.

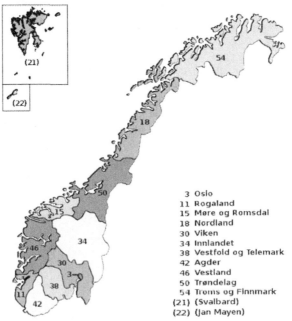

3 Oslo
11 Rogaland
15 Møre og Romsdal
18 Nordland
30 Viken
34 Innlandet
38 Vestfold og Telemark
42 Agder
46 Vestland
50 Trøndelag
54 Troms og Finnmark
(21) (Svalbard)
(22) (Jan Mayen)

Beyond the postcard-perfect beauty lies a captivating medley of geography, regions, and counties, each holding unique stories and adventures waiting to be unraveled.[2]

This chapter is your introductory map, guiding you through the heart and soul of Norway. It'll paint a vivid picture of its breathtaking landscapes, from the jagged peaks of the north to the sun-drenched archipelagoes of the south. It'll introduce you to its rich history, from the stoic Vikings to the modern-day pioneers of sustainable living. It'll even demystify the quirks of Norwegian culture, from the reserved charm of its people to the unique concept of "hygge," the art of cozy contentment.

A Land Forged by Ice and Fjords

Norway, an ethereal blend of jagged mountains, shimmering fjords, and coastal towns, is a land where nature reigns supreme. But beyond the postcard-perfect beauty lies a captivating medley of geography, regions, and counties, each holding unique stories and adventures waiting to be unraveled. It's time to embark on a journey, traversing the country's diverse landscapes and uncovering the soul of this Nordic nation.

- **Sculpted by Glaciers:** Norway's dramatic topography is a testament to the sculpting power of ancient glaciers. The iconic fjords, deep cuts in the land carved by retreating ice, snake through the mountainous landscapes, offering breathtaking fjord-side drives and serene kayaking adventures. From the majestic Sognefjord, the longest in Norway, to the dramatic Geirangerfjord, a UNESCO World Heritage Site, these watery wonders are the country's lifeblood, shaping its coastline and fostering vibrant fishing communities.

- **Kingdom of Regions:** Norway is traditionally divided into five distinct regions, each with its own character and charm. In the south, you'll find Sørlandet, where sun-kissed beaches and laid-back vibes welcome sunseekers. The Eastern Fjords region boasts soaring mountains, villages, and the historic city of Bergen, a gateway to the enchanting fjords. Further north lies Trøndelag, a land of lush valleys, vibrant festivals, and the majestic Nidaros Cathedral, a masterpiece of Gothic architecture.

- **Western Norway:** The land of glaciers and waterfalls beckons with dramatic scenery and endless outdoor adventures. Hiking amidst the snow-capped peaks of the Jotunheimen National Park or kayaking amid the azure waters of the Geirangerfjord are experiences that etch themselves onto your soul. In the far north, Northern Norway unveils another world where the Arctic Circle kisses the land, painting the skies with the magic of the Aurora Borealis and offering glimpses of polar bears and reindeer.

- **A Puzzle of Counties:** Each region comprises counties with distinct identities and cultural nuances. Akershus in Eastern Norway is home to the bustling capital, Oslo, while Telemark boasts wooden stave churches and a rich folk tradition. In Western Norway, Møre og Romsdal's dramatic coastline gives way to fertile valleys and captivating waterfalls, while in the north, Troms and Finnmark offer stark beauty, Sami culture, and the thrill of chasing the Aurora Borealis.

- **Beyond the Fjords:** While Norway's dramatic landscapes are its undoubted crown jewels, its cultural and historical fusion is equally captivating. Vibrant cities like Oslo and Bergen offer museums, art galleries, and a thriving culinary scene. Quaint coastal villages whisper tales of Viking history and maritime traditions, while quaint mountain towns invite you to cozy up by crackling fireplaces and savor local delicacies.

- **Untamed and Unforgettable:** Whether you're a seasoned adventurer, a nature enthusiast, or a seeker of cultural immersion, Norway has something for everyone. Hike through untouched wilderness, kayak through fjords, or cycle along scenic coastal routes. Discover Viking relics, dive into medieval history, or lose yourself in the warmth of local hospitality.

If you're searching for a land where nature paints an awe-inspiring canvas, ancient stories mingle with modern charm, and adventure awaits around every bend, then Norway is calling. Remember, this is just a glimpse into the captivating world of Norway. Each region, county, and town offers unique experiences waiting to be discovered. So, start planning your Nordic adventure and experience the magic of Norway for yourself.

Echoes of Vikings and Fjords: A Journey through Norwegian History

Norway, a land where wind-swept mountains embrace shimmering fjords, boasts a history as dramatic and captivating as its landscape. From the thunderous sagas of Vikings to the quiet resilience of farmers battling harsh winters, each chapter of Norway's past has shaped the nation you know today. So, grab your mead horn and journey through time, unraveling the key events and figures that have forged the soul of Norway.

- **Viking Voyages:** Norway's story begins with the roar of longships slicing through icy waters. The era of the Vikings, from 800 to 1050 AD, saw these fierce seafarers leave their indelible mark on Norway. Led by figures like Harald Fairhair, who unified the country in the 9th century, and Erik the Red, who ventured to Greenland and Iceland, the Vikings carved their legacy through exploration, trade, and (to be honest) some rather aggressive raids. Their sagas, infused with mythical creatures and tales of bravery, still echo in Norway's folklore and national identity.

- **A Crown, a Conversion, and a Black Death:** The Viking Age gave way to a period of consolidation and Christianization. Olaf Haraldsson – later canonized as Saint Olav – brought Christianity to Norway in the 10th century, unifying the country under a single faith. He tragically met his end at the Battle of Stiklestad in 1030, but his legacy as a unifying figure and martyr resonates throughout Norwegian history. However, the Middle Ages weren't all sunshine and sermons. The Black Death swept across Europe in 1347, devastating Norway and leaving a lasting scar on the country's population and social fabric.

- **Union and Independence:** The following centuries saw Norway embroiled in a complex dance of alliances and power struggles. In 1380, it entered a 434-year union with Denmark, followed by a turbulent century under Swedish rule in the 19th century. Yet, throughout these periods of external control, the embers of Norwegian independence flickered. Figures like Henrik Wergeland, a fiery poet and political activist, and the composer Edvard Grieg, whose music captured the soul of the land, nurtured a growing sense of national identity.

- **A Nation Awakens:** In 1905, Norway regained its independence by peacefully dissolving its union with Sweden. This pivotal moment, fueled by the unwavering spirit of the Norwegian people, ushered in a new era of self-determination and progress. The following decades saw Norway blossom into a prosperous and forward-thinking nation, embracing democracy, social welfare, and a unique brand of quiet patriotism.

- **Modern Norway:** Today, Norway is an outstanding example of environmental consciousness, social equality, and technological innovation. Yet, the echoes of its rich past continue to resonate. From the Viking ship replicas gracing Oslo's harbor to the ancient stave churches dotting the countryside, Norwegians proudly celebrate their heritage.

- **More Than Just Fjords and Fjords:** As you stand awestruck before a cascading waterfall or wander through a coastal village, remember that Norway's beauty is only half the story. It's a land shaped by the courage of Vikings, the faith of a king, and the unwavering spirit of a people who fought for their independence. To truly understand Norway, you must uncover its past, let its myths and legends wash over you, and witness how the echoes of history continue to shape the vibrant nation it is today.

Ready to embark on your Norwegian adventure? Start by exploring these fascinating historical sites:

- **Viking Ship Museum, Oslo:** Witness the fearsome longships of the Viking era and learn about their maritime prowess.

- **Nidaros Cathedral, Trondheim:** A masterpiece of Gothic and Romanesque architecture, this cathedral was the coronation church of Norwegian kings for centuries.

- **Bryggen Wharf, Bergen:** Step back in time with these colorful wooden houses, remnants of Bergen's medieval trading past.

- **Maihaugen Open-Air Museum, Lillehammer:** Discover traditional Norwegian life through authentic houses, workshops, and historical reenactments.

- **Polar Museum, Tromsø:** Learn about the history of Arctic exploration and the resilient communities that have thrived in these harsh conditions.

Norway's rich history awaits you. Unravel its threads and discover the soul of a nation sculpted by adventure, resilience, and the boundless beauty of its landscapes.

Embracing the Elements: Weather, Packing, and Natural Hazards

Norway, the land of majestic fjords and snow-capped peaks, casts a spell of awe-inspiring beauty. But before you embark on your Nordic adventure, understanding the country's unique climate and weather patterns is crucial. From packing the right gear to navigating potential natural hazards, this section will help you prepare to embrace the elements and make the most of your journey.

Seasons of Enchantment: Norway's seasons' are made up of a diverse palette.

- **Winter (December-February):** Embrace the magical world of a winter wonderland. Crisp air, snow-covered landscapes, and the ethereal glow of the northern lights make for unforgettable experiences. However, be prepared for freezing temperatures, icy roads, and limited daylight hours. Pack thermals, layers, waterproof boots, and a warm winter coat. Consider winter sports like skiing, snowshoeing, or dog sledding.

- **Spring (March-May):** Witness the dramatic thaw. Melting snow reveals vibrant green valleys, cascading waterfalls roar to life, and daylight hours lengthen. Temperatures remain chilly, so layered clothing with rain gear is still essential. Hiking, cycling, and fjord cruises are perfect ways to enjoy the blossoming landscape.

- **Summer (June-August):** Soak in the golden glow of long summer days. Enjoy warm temperatures, vibrant wildflowers, and endless daylight (north of the Arctic Circle, experience the midnight sun). Pack for warmer weather, comfortable shoes, and swimwear for those refreshing fjord dips. Hiking, kayaking, and camping are ideal summer activities.

- **Autumn (September-November):** Witness a colorful transformation. Golden hues paint the forests, crisp air invigorates, and harvest festivals abound. Pack for cooler temperatures and potential rain. Hiking, sightseeing, and enjoying cozy cafes are perfect autumn pursuits.

Natural Wonders, Natural Threats: While Norway's beauty is undeniable, certain natural hazards deserve awareness.

- **Avalanches:** Be especially cautious in mountainous regions during winter and spring. Research avalanche forecasts and follow safety guidelines provided by local authorities.

- **Rockslides:** Similar to avalanches, you should be mindful of potential rockfalls, especially after heavy rain or snowmelt.

- **Flash Floods:** Heavy rainfall triggers sudden flooding, particularly in valleys and coastal areas. Stay informed about weather warnings and avoid low-lying areas during storms.

- **Storms and Strong Winds:** Coastal areas experience strong winds and storms, especially in winter. Check weather forecasts and exercise caution near the ocean during rough conditions.

Packing Like a Viking: Gear up for adventure with these tips:

- **Layers Are Your Friend:** Adapt to variable temperatures by packing clothes you can easily layer and remove.

- **Footwear Matters:** Invest in sturdy, waterproof hiking boots or shoes for uneven terrain. Pack warmer boots for winter travel.

- **Embrace Rain, Embrace Sunshine:** Pack a rain jacket and waterproof backpack to prepare for unpredictable weather. Don't forget sunglasses and sunscreen for those sunny days.

- **Be Prepared for Emergencies:** Include a first-aid kit, headlamp, and emergency blanket in your backpack. Download essential offline maps and emergency contact information.

- **Embrace the Unpredictable:** Remember, part of Norway's charm lies in its unpredictable weather. Embrace the occasional downpour as a chance to cozy up in a cafe with a hot drink. Adapt your plans based on the elements and focus on enjoying each season's unique adventures.

Always check local weather forecasts and safety guidelines before embarking on any outdoor activities in Norway. Go forth, Viking-in-the-making, armed with knowledge and respect for the elements. Norway awaits, ready to unfold its breathtaking beauty, one season, one fjord, one awe-inspiring moment at a time.

Fjord and Friluftsliv: Unveiling the Heartbeat of Norwegian Culture

Norway, the land of the midnight sun and cascading waterfalls isn't just a majestic landscape.[3]

Norway, the land of the midnight sun and cascading waterfalls, isn't just a majestic landscape; it's a symphony of captivating culture, vibrant traditions, and a unique way of life woven into the very fabric of its society. From the stoicism of its people to the vibrant festivals that burst onto the scene, embracing Norwegian culture is an essential part of any Nordic adventure.

Friluftsliv: A Love Affair with Nature

At the heart of Norwegian culture lies "friluftsliv," a cherished concept that translates to "life in the open air." Norwegians are intrinsically connected to their wilderness, whether hiking snow-capped peaks, kayaking through fjords, or simply picnicking in a sun-dappled forest. Embrace this love for nature, pack your hiking boots, and immerse yourself in the invigorating beauty of the outdoors.

Cozy Hygge and Quiet Respect

Don't mistake Norwegian reserve for coldness. The concept of "hygge" embodies the warmth and contentment found in simple things such as flickering candles, shared stories, and cozy moments with loved ones.

While Norwegians value their privacy and personal space, their warmth shines through in genuine smiles and helpful gestures. Respect this quiet demeanor, let conversations unfold naturally, and embrace the simple joys of "hygge."

Samí Culture: A Tapestry of Resilience

In the far north, the vibrant culture of the Samí people, the indigenous inhabitants of Arctic Norway, adds another layer to the country's tapestry. Renowned for their tradition of reindeer herding, intricate handicrafts, and rich storytelling, the Samí offer a particular window into resilience and a deep connection to the land. Immerse yourself in their culture by visiting a traditional Samí "goahti" dwelling, savoring reindeer stew, or appreciating their captivating joik singing.

Festivals and Celebrations

Norwegians know how to celebrate. From the joyous revelry of Constitution Day on May 17th, with vibrant parades and children's marches, to the cozy bonfire gatherings of Midsummer, Norway's calendar is dotted with colorful festivities. Don't miss the Bergen International Festival, a vibrant celebration of music, or the quirky Tromsø International Film Festival, where movies play under the midnight sun.

Cultural Etiquette: Navigating the Social Seas

To navigate the cultural waters smoothly, remember these rules of thumb:

- **Greetings and Titles:** "Hei" is the informal "hello," while "God dag" is more formal. Respect titles like "Herr" (Mr.) and "Fru" (Mrs.).

- **Punctuality Is Key:** Norwegians value timeliness. Arrive on time for appointments and social gatherings.

- **Shoes off Indoors:** When visiting someone's home, remove your shoes at the door.

- **Let the Host Take the Lead:** Don't overstep boundaries. Wait for your host to offer food, drinks, or directions.

- **Embrace Silence:** Norwegians appreciate quiet moments. Don't feel the need to fill every pause in conversation.

Beyond the Fjords

Norway isn't just about stunning scenery. It's about understanding the soul of its people. By understanding the nuances of their culture, traditions, and etiquette, you'll forge deeper connections and experience Norway from the inside out. You'll discover a land where nature inspires, history whispers, and warm hearts beat beneath a serene Nordic sky.

From Fjord to Flavor: A Taste of Norway's Artful Delights

Beyond the breathtaking fjords and snow-capped peaks, Norway whispers a tale of culture woven into every bite and brushstroke. It's time for a sensory journey through this Nordic nation, where tradition takes center stage in both the kitchen and the workshop.

- **A Culinary Canvas:** Norwegian cuisine is an ode to the land's bounty. Fresh seafood, like fjord-kissed salmon and plump mussels, takes center stage, often paired with creamy sauces and pickled vegetables. Hearty stews, simmered with reindeer or lamb, warm you from within on crisp evenings. And don't forget brunost, the addictive brown cheese slathered on crispbread. It's a sweet-savory symbol of Norwegian comfort food.

- **Beyond the Palate:** It's not just the plethora of food; art and crafts flow like molten lava from the creative heart of Norway. Viking-inspired wood carvings adorn houses, while intricate rosemaling paints stories on furniture and traditional *bunad* costumes. Be mesmerized by the hypnotic rhythms of the Hardanger fiddle, a national treasure born in the depths of the fjords.

- **Regional Rhythms:** Each region boasts its culinary symphony. Bergen welcomes you with creamy fish soup and aromatic seafood chowder. Head north to Trondheim and savor succulent cured reindeer meat, a legacy of Sami traditions. In the south, sun-drenched farms offer juicy berries and sweet pastries, perfect for lazy afternoons by the fjord.

- **Crafting Memories:** Take a piece of Norway back with you. Learn the art of *kniplinger,* a delicate lacemaking passed down through generations. Weave your own Viking bracelet or carve a miniature troll, a mischievous souvenir of your Nordic adventure.

- **A Nordic Invitation:** Norway is a place to savor, feel, and experience. Raise a toast to fresh fjords and intense flavors. Let the traditional tunes dance in your ears, and let the artistry of this enchanting land become a permanent part of your story.

Norway's cultural treasures are waiting to be unearthed. Be an active participant, not just a spectator. Embrace the flavors, sights, and sounds, and discover the soul of this nation, one bite, one brushstroke, one melody at a time.

Navigate Norway Like a Viking: Conquering the Fjords and Beyond

Norway's majestic landscapes beckon, waterfalls roaring like battle cries, fjords stretching like sapphire pathways, and villages clinging to cliff faces like mythical strongholds. But how do you navigate this breathtaking kingdom? Fear not, intrepid traveler, for Norway's transportation system, like a well-oiled Viking longship, is ready to whisk you through every fjord and mountain pass.

- **Trains Like Thunderbolts:** Norway's trains are marvels of engineering, carving their way through valleys, hugging coastlines, and offering you panoramic views that will leave you breathless. The iconic Bergen Railway snakes through snow-capped mountains, the Oslo-Trondheim line zips past enchanted forests, and the Nordland Line unveils the Arctic Circle's icy grandeur. Purchase tickets online or at stations, validate them before boarding, and settle in for a journey that's as much about the sights as the destination.

- **Buses for Every Fjord:** Norway's extensive network connects even the most remote corners, from sleek express coaches to village buses. Download the Skyss app for real-time schedules and ticketing, or use the Ruter system in Oslo and Bergen. Remember, cash is king in smaller villages, so stock up on those kroner.

- **Ferries: Fjord Kings of the Sea:** No Norwegian adventure is complete without a fjord-faring ferry ride. These vessels, from sleek catamarans to rugged car ferries, are lifelines and scenic cruises in one. Board at bustling harbors or tiny village piers, watch the cliffs rise above the water's edge, and breathe in the salty air. Tickets can be purchased on board or online, and some even offer onboard cafes for a taste of local seafood while you sail.

- **Bikes and Boots for the Adventurous Soul:** Rent a bicycle, explore coastal villages, or lace up your hiking boots and conquer mountain trails. Norway's vast network of bike paths and hiking routes cater to every fitness level, ranging from gentle coastal strolls to challenging mountain ascents.

- **Beyond the Wheels:** Don't forget the magic of walking. Explore towns, discover hidden waterfalls, and soak up the local atmosphere on foot. Norway is a pedestrian paradise, and its beauty unfolds best at a leisurely pace.

Tips for Transit Triumph:

- Remember to validate train tickets
- Download the Skyss app for bus schedules and ticketing
- Pack snacks for longer journeys, especially on buses
- Be prepared for weather changes, even on a short trip
- Relax, enjoy the scenery, and let the journey be part of the adventure

Do you feel a sense of excitement and anticipation should tingle through your spine? You've taken the first step towards unlocking the magic of Norway, gaining a deeper understanding of its landscapes, culture, and practicalities. Remember, this is just the beginning.

Each subsequent chapter explores specific regions, offering specialized itineraries, hidden gems, and insider tips to tailor your adventure. But even before you turn the page, a transformation has begun. You've awakened the Viking spirit within, a thirst for exploration, a hunger for adventure, and a yearning to connect with the soul of this captivating country.

So, *go forth, Viking*, with your newfound knowledge and awakened spirit. Embrace the challenge of unfamiliar landscapes, the warmth of welcoming smiles, and the thrill of new experiences. Norway awaits, and with this guide as your compass, you're ready to write your unforgettable Nordic saga!

Chapter 2: To and From the Airport

Norway awaits your arrival with its breathtaking landscapes, captivating culture, and endless outdoor adventures. But before you're immersed in the land of fjords and Viking lore, conquering the logistical hurdle of airport transportation needs to be tackled. Fear not, intrepid traveler. This chapter is your compass, guiding you through the various options to seamlessly navigate your way from the airport tarmac to the heart of your Norwegian adventure.

Your Guide to Oslo Airport Gardermoen (OSL)

Oslo Airport Gardermoen (OSL) is a portal to Nordic magic.'

Oslo Airport Gardermoen (OSL) is a portal to Nordic magic. Nestled 48 kilometers northeast of Oslo, its two terminals welcome you with a warm embrace. The two terminals are integrated, so you can access your flight gate easily. Whether you're a seasoned adventurer or a wide-eyed explorer, it's time to unlock the secrets of OSL and begin your journey with an unforgettable experience.

Terminal 2: A Design Fjord Where Vikings Roam

Stepping into Terminal 2 is like entering a contemporary Nordic saga. Sunlight bathes the central hall, illuminating travelers from around the world. As you weave through the throngs of other visitors, the aroma of freshly brewed coffee from Ritazza mingles with scents of the perfumes you can find at Travel Value, reminding you of the journey that awaits.

OSL is more than just a logistical marvel. It's a cultural canvas. Dive into N°rth, where you can find an array of souvenirs, trolls, knitwear, and viking products. Or explore the OSL Gallery, where contemporary Norwegian artists showcase their bold visions on canvas and sculpture.

Beyond the Basics:

For the curious soul, Terminal 2 offers a treasure trove of experiences that transcend the ordinary:

- **Indulge in a Nordic Spa Ritual:** Pamper yourself at the Be Relax Spa in the airport, where saunas and rejuvenating treatments embrace you in Nordic comfort. Emerge feeling invigorated and ready to tackle glaciers and climb snow-capped peaks.

- **Become a Mini-Explorer:** Embark on a self-guided "Art on the Move" tour through the terminal. Discover hidden sculptures and paintings strategically placed amidst the sleek architecture, transforming your journey into an unexpected art extravaganza.

- **Catch the Northern Lights in a Flash:** If your travels coincide with the long winter nights, consider booking a two-hour flight to Trømso from OSL. Soar above the clouds and witness the mesmerizing spectacle of the Aurora Borealis flashing across the Arctic sky. It's a memory that will forever light up your soul.

Terminal 1: Where Charm Meets Convenience:

While Terminal 2 boasts modern splendor, Terminal 1 exudes a warm, familiar charm. Its layout is easy to navigate, with baggage claim, information desks, and currency exchange readily accessible. Trains whisk you away to Norwegian towns, while buses connect you to vibrant cities like Bergen and Trondheim.

While Terminal 2 boasts modern splendor, Terminal 1 exudes a warm, familiar charm.[5]

Unveiling Local Gems:

More than a gateway to domestic flights, Terminal 1 is a window into local life:

- **Savor the Flavors of Norway:** The Food Court is a symphony of aromas, from freshly hveteboller (sweet cardamom rolls) to steaming *fiskesuppe* (fish soup) bowls. Grab a quick bite or linger over a leisurely meal, savoring the taste of local delicacies.

- **Discover Hidden Treasures:** Browse shops brimming with souvenirs, from hand-knit sweaters adorned with Viking runes to intricately carved wooden trolls. Each item whispers a story of Norwegian craftsmanship, allowing you to carry a piece of the country home.

- **Take a Trip Back in Time:** The Norwegian Armed Forces Aircraft Collection awaits just outside the terminal. Explore vintage aircraft, from biplanes to fighter jets, and learn about Norway's rich aviation history.

Beyond the Airport Walls:

OSL's magic extends far beyond its gleaming terminals. Take a quick hop on the Flytoget high-speed train, and in just 19 minutes, you'll be strolling down Oslo's vibrant Karl Johans gate. Explore the Akershus

Fortress, marvel at the Munch Museum's iconic "The Scream," or sail the Oslofjord on a traditional wooden boat. Venture further into the countryside and discover villages nestled amidst emerald valleys, breathtaking fjords carving through rugged landscapes, and snow-capped mountains that whisper tales of Vikings and trolls.

Embrace the Nordic spirit, navigate the friendly terminals of OSL, and step beyond the runways into an adventure that awaits. From the sleek design of Terminal 2 to the warm charm of Terminal 1, Oslo Airport Gardermoen is a gateway not just to Norway but to a world of unforgettable experiences. Let the magic begin.

Unveiling Your Next Journey from OSL

Oslo Airport Gardermoen (OSL), set amidst emerald forests and fjords beckoning on the horizon, is a portal to adventures that crackle with Viking spirit. However, navigating your next chapter can feel like deciphering a cryptic rune stone. It's time to unveil the secrets to a seamless departure, ensuring your next destination awaits with open arms, whether you seek urban buzz, serene landscapes, or the thrill of the open road.

Train: The Red Rocket to Oslo's Heart

Step out of the terminal and let your eyes scan for the fiery red streak, the Airport Express Train. This sleek chariot whisks you directly to Oslo Central Station in a mere 19 minutes, making it the fastest and most frequent option during peak hours. Trains depart every 10 minutes, a rhythmic beat against the anticipation of your arrival.

Embarking on the Red Journey:

1. **Tickets:** Purchase online for convenience, at ticket machines in the airport, or onboard the trains. Consider the Oslo Pass for unlimited travel on public transport within your chosen validity period, a passport to the city's vibrant pulse.

2. **Platforms:** Look for signs directing you to the Airport Express Train platforms. Validate your ticket before boarding, a small ritual before the adventure begins.

3. **Seating:** Choose from standard seats or first-class comfort, complete with luggage compartments and power sockets for your weary devices. Relax, watch the scenery blur past, and arrive refreshed in the heart of Oslo, ready to conquer its cobbled streets and cultural treasures.

Tips for a Smooth Ride:

- Download the NSB app for real-time train schedules and ticket purchases, ensuring you never miss a beat.

- Consider the regional train service for connections to other Norwegian cities, expanding your Nordic adventure.

- Validate your ticket before boarding to avoid fines. It's a small price for a smooth journey.

Bus: Exploring Beyond the City Walls

Flybussen, a network of bright yellow buses, offers a flexible and budget-friendly option for reaching destinations within Oslo and nearby towns. Choose your desired service based on your budget and destination. Take express routes for a swifter journey to specific landmarks or regional routes for a wider reach, weaving your path through villages and picturesque landscapes.

Navigating the Flybussen Network:

1. **Ticketing:** Purchase online for the best deals at Flybussen ticket machines in the airport or onboard the bus. Consider multi-day tickets for unlimited travel on Flybussen routes within your chosen validity period, a cost-effective way to explore the region.

2. **Bus Stops:** Look for the designated Flybussen stops outside both terminals, clearly marked with your desired destinations. Don't worry; the friendly yellow giants are hard to miss.

3. **Boarding:** Validate your ticket before boarding and find your designated seat. Enjoy the comfortable ride and soak in the changing scenery, from the airport's sleek exterior to villages nestled amidst rolling hills.

Flybussen Tips:

- Check the Flybussen website for detailed route maps and schedules to plan your journey with precision.

- Consider multi-day tickets for unlimited travel on Flybussen routes within your timeframe.

- Pack light, as luggage space might be limited on certain routes, leaving room for souvenirs and memories to fill.

Taxi: Door-to-Door Convenience

For a touch of luxury and effortless arrival, taxis stand at your service outside both terminals. This option is ideal for late-night arrivals, large groups, or destinations not well-served by public transport, ensuring you reach your doorstep with ease.

Flagging a Yellow Chariot:

1. Head to the designated taxi queue outside the terminal. Taxis are readily available and metered, ensuring fair pricing. No need to hail in the Nordic wind; simply wait your turn and let the yellow chariot whisk you away!

2. Inform the driver of your destination. They are familiar with the city and surrounding areas, and local experts are ready to guide you through the urban labyrinth.

3. Relax and enjoy the ride directly to your doorstep. Watch the city lights dance past as you settle into the rhythm of your new adventure.

Taxi Tips:

- Download a ride-hailing app like Uber for booking and fare estimates, especially if your Norwegian isn't entirely up to par.

- Consider sharing a taxi with fellow travelers to split the cost. It's also a chance to forge new friendships.

- Carry enough cash, as not all taxis accept credit cards.

Car Rental: Your Viking Chariot Awaits

If you crave the freedom of the open road, several car rental companies operate desks within both OSL terminals. Choose your chariot to conquer Norway's breathtaking landscapes, from sleek city cars to rugged SUVs. Before you zoom off like a modern-day Viking, remember these tips:

Claiming Your Wheels:

1. **Booking:** Pre-book online for the best deals and ensure your preferred vehicle is available, especially during peak season. Alternatively, choose from a variety of cars upon arrival.

2. **Documentation:** Pack your valid driver's license, passport, and any necessary travel documents. International drivers might require an International Driving Permit.

3. **Insurance:** Consider additional insurance options for peace of mind, especially if venturing off the beaten path.

Navigating Norway's Roads:

- **Toll Roads:** Be aware of potential toll roads on certain routes. Download the AutoPASS app for automatic toll payments, ensuring a smooth journey without the hassle of stopping at booths.

- **Road Rules:** Familiarize yourself with Norwegian traffic regulations, including mandatory headlights even during daylight hours and speed limits that might differ from your home country.

- **Rest Stops:** Embrace the *hytte* culture (the idea of staying outdoors, enjoying small cabins out in the countryside). Make pit stops at rest areas with cozy cafes, scenic overlooks, and even playgrounds for weary travelers. Pack a picnic lunch and enjoy the fresh Nordic air as you recharge for the next leg of your journey.

Car Rental Tips:

- Consider fuel efficiency, especially if you're planning longer journeys. Electric car rentals are becoming increasingly available, a sustainable way to explore the country.

- Download offline maps and navigation apps, preparing for unexpected detours or areas with limited internet connectivity.

- Leave no trace. Respect the pristine beauty of Norway and dispose of waste responsibly.

Regardless of your vehicle, departing OSL is a gateway to endless adventures. Choose your path – whether the sleek speed of the train, the vibrant medley of the Flybussen network, the comfort of a taxi's door-to-door service, or the open road freedom of a rental car. *Let the Scandinavian spirit guide you.* Explore and conquer your next chapter from OSL, for the journey is just as enchanting as the destination.

Beyond Oslo: Norway's Regional Airports

While Oslo Gardermoen (OSL) is the main gateway to Norway, venturing beyond its sleek terminals unlocks a treasure trove of regional airports. Each airport is a portal to unique landscapes, vibrant cities, and captivating experiences. From the sun-kissed fjords of the west to the Arctic wonders of the north, these airports offer a kaleidoscope of adventures, waiting to paint your Norwegian journey with unforgettable memories.

Bergen Airport, Flesland (BGO): Where History Lingers amidst Fjords

Step off the plane at Bergen Airport (BGO) and inhale the fresh sea air. It's a prelude to the vibrant "City of Rain" found among verdant mountains and the glistening Byfjorden. Stroll through the UNESCO-listed Bryggen harbor, where colorful wooden houses whisper tales of Hanseatic merchants and bustling fish markets. Climb aboard the Fløibanen funicular for panoramic views that will leave you breathless, or delve into the rich musical heritage of Edvard Grieg at his enchanting Troldhaugen home.

Beyond BGO:

- **Light Rail:** Your transport to Bergen city center in 20 minutes, a seamless transition from airport bustle to urban charm.

- **Buses:** Punctual buses will weave you through villages and dramatic landscapes, connecting you to nearby towns and hidden gems.

- **Car Rentals:** Embrace the freedom of the open road and explore the majestic fjords, quaint fishing villages, and hidden waterfalls of western Norway at your own pace.

- **Ferries:** Set sail on an adventure! Island-hopping across the picturesque archipelago unveils secluded coves, untouched beaches, and postcard-perfect villages.

Stavanger Airport, Sola (SVG): Where Vikings Danced under the Midnight Sun

Stavanger Airport (SVG) welcomes you to the Land of the Midnight Sun, a vibrant city bathed in sunshine and Viking spirit. Explore the Old Town, where cobbled streets and colorful wooden houses tell tales of a bygone era. Climb the Pulpit Rock, a natural marvel that has mesmerized adventurers for centuries, and witness the Lysefjord unfold like a breathtaking canvas beneath your feet.

Beyond SVG:

- **Flybussen:** Your swift shuttle to Stavanger city center in about 25 minutes, ensuring a quick transition from touchdown to urban exploration.

- **Buses:** Venture beyond the city limits and discover the dramatic coastline, pristine beaches, and fishing villages dotting the southwestern Norwegian landscape.

- **Car Rentals:** Unwind on secluded beaches, kayak through hidden coves, and chase waterfalls along the rugged coastline. With a rental car, the adventures are limitless.

- **Ferries:** Embark on a fjord odyssey. The Lysefjord beckons with its emerald waters and towering cliffs, while countless other fjords promise stunning scenery and unforgettable experiences.

Trondheim Airport, Værnes (TRD): Where History Meets Vibrant Culture

Trondheim Airport (TRD) is your gateway to the "City of Nidaros," a cultural hub nestled amidst the fjords and mountains of central Norway. Explore the majestic Nidaros Cathedral, a masterpiece of Gothic architecture that whispers tales of medieval bishops and Viking kings. Wander through the lively Bakklandet district, where independent shops and colorful houses exude a bohemian charm. Discover the rich Viking history at the Sverresborg Trøndelag Folkemuseum.

Beyond TRD:

- **Airport Express Train:** Your sleek chariot whisks you directly to Trondheim city center in just 35 minutes, ensuring a hassle-free arrival.

- **Buses:** Venture beyond the city limits and discover the villages, dramatic fjords, and untouched wilderness that define central Norway.

- **Car Rentals:** Trace the Trondheimsfjord, a scenic ribbon of water, or chase the Northern Lights across the Arctic Circle.

- **Trains and Buses:** Hop on a train or bus and explore the Arctic wonders of Tromsø, Kirkenes, and beyond, where snow-capped mountains and vibrant Sami culture await.

Tromsø Airport, Langnes (TOS): Chasing the Aurora in the Arctic Wonderland

Tromsø Airport (TOS) is your portal to the Arctic wonderland of northern Norway. It's a land where snow-capped mountains pierce the sky, the dazzling Northern Lights dance across the winter nights, and vibrant Sami culture warms the soul. Experience the thrill of dog sledding across frozen landscapes or conquer the majestic Lyngen Alps on guided ski tours. In the summer, witness the midnight sun paint the sky in vibrant hues, kayak through icy fjords, and hike under endless daylight.

Beyond TOS:

- **Flybussen and Taxis:** These are your go-to rides for Tromsø city center, ensuring a quick transition from Arctic chill to urban warmth.

- **Buses and Trains:** Venture beyond the city limits and explore the dramatic fjords, untouched wilderness, and fishing villages dotting the northern coastline.

- **Car Rentals:** Embark on an Arctic road trip. Navigate winding roads towards secluded bays, chase the Northern Lights across vast landscapes, and experience the magic of Norway's far north at your own pace.

- **Hurtigruten Cruises:** Sail the iconic coastal route. This legendary ship connects Tromsø with numerous ports, offering a unique perspective on the Arctic wonderland and a chance to delve into local culture.

Bodø Airport (BOO): Where Mountains Meet the Sea in Rugged Splendor

Bodø Airport (BOO) welcomes you to a land where jagged mountains plunge into the icy embrace of the Norwegian Sea. It's a landscape sculpted by glaciers and Viking legends. Hike to the summit of Saltstraumen, a swirling maelstrom that mesmerizes onlookers, or delve into the rich Viking history at the Bodø Saltstraumen Museum. In the summer, the midnight sun flashes across the sky or kayak through hidden coves teeming with birdlife.

Beyond BOO:

- **Buses and Taxis:** Your trusty transport to navigate Bodø city center and explore the surrounding villages and dramatic coastline.

- **Car Rentals:** Embrace the freedom of the open road and conquer the Lofoten Islands, a breathtaking archipelago of jagged peaks, secluded beaches, and fishing villages.

- **Hurtigruten Cruises:** This legendary ship connects Bodø with other Nordic gems, offering a unique perspective on the rugged coastline and a chance to experience local charm.

- **Ferries:** Hop aboard and island-hop. Discover hidden coves, pristine beaches, and untouched wilderness on the numerous islands that dot the Bodø region.

Alesund Airport, Vigra (AES): Where Art Deco Dances with Viking Charm

Alesund Airport (AES) whisks you into a fairytale city, where Art Deco buildings line colorful canals. It's reminiscent of a miniature Amsterdam nestled amidst stunning fjords. Explore the UNESCO-listed town center, a delightful maze of shops, cafes, and architectural gems. Climb Fjellstua for panoramic views or embark on a fjord cruise to witness waterfalls cascading down towering cliffs.

Beyond AES:

- **Buses and Taxis:** Your convenient connections to Alesund city center and nearby villages ensure a seamless transition from airport hustle to exploration.

- **Car Rentals:** Drive along the dramatic Atlantic Road, a serpentine ribbon of asphalt that snakes between islands and offers breathtaking ocean vistas.

- **Ferries:** Island-hopping adventures await. Discover untouched beaches, hidden coves, and fishing villages on the Alesund region's numerous islands.

- **Hiking and Kayaking:** Lace up your boots or grab your paddle. Numerous trails and waterways offer endless opportunities to explore the stunning landscapes surrounding Alesund.

Alta Airport (ALF): Where the Aurora Borealis Paints the Arctic Sky

Alta Airport (ALF) is your gateway to the Arctic frontier, a land where the Northern Lights dance across the winter sky, reindeer roam the untouched wilderness, and Sami culture thrives. Visit the Sorrisniva Igloo Hotel, carved from snow and ice, or chase the elusive Northern Lights on guided tours. In the summer, hike through wildflower-carpeted meadows, kayak through glacial fjords, and witness the midnight sun paint the sky in vibrant hues.

Beyond ALF:

- **Buses and Taxis:** Your reliable connections to Alta city center and nearby villages. They ensure a hassle-free arrival in this Arctic wonderland.

- **Car Rentals:** Conquer the Finnmark region at your own pace. Drive along the Arctic Highway, witness dramatic landscapes, and discover hidden gems off the beaten path.

- **Dog Sledding and Snowshoeing:** Embrace the ancient Arctic spirit. Experience the thrill of dog sledding across frozen landscapes or explore the untouched wilderness on snowshoes.

- **Northern Lights Safaris:** Join guided tours and chase the mesmerizing Aurora Borealis across the vast Arctic sky, a spectacle that will leave you awestruck!

This glimpse into Norway's regional airports is just the beginning. Each one offers a unique gateway to a specific facet of this enchanting country, promising experiences that will resonate in your soul long after your journey ends.

Oslo Gardermoen (OSL) may be the gateway to Norway, but it's also a portal to endless possibilities. Choose the sleek speed of the train, the vibrant yellow odyssey of the Flybussen, the door-to-door convenience of a taxi, or the freedom of your own Viking chariot. OSL is the launchpad for adventures that will paint your Norwegian journey with unforgettable memories. So, step out of the terminal, embrace the crisp Nordic air, and embark on your next chapter, knowing the treasure – the journey itself – is a gem waiting to be discovered!

Chapter 3: Oslo: Norway's Capital

Oslo, the beating heart of Norway, is a vibrant mosaic crafted from Viking whispers and contemporary cool. This bustling capital city is a gateway to stunning fjords and snow-capped mountains. It's also a cultural powerhouse, a design haven, and a foodie paradise waiting to be savored.

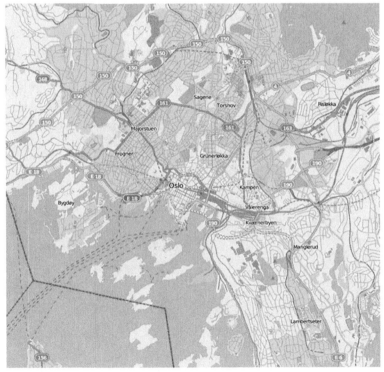

Oslo on the map.[6]

Whether you're chasing Viking ghosts in ancient fortresses or marveling at futuristic masterpieces, Oslo has something for every explorer. Prepare to trade your travel socks for comfy shoes because you'll journey through the city's history, culture, and must-see tourist spots. It's a tour that will leave you captivated by Oslo's charm. Buckle up, fellow adventurer.

Oslo Unveiled: Navigating the Fjord Capital Like a Viking

Oslo boasts neighborhoods, historical districts, and the shimmering embrace of the Oslofjord. For first-time visitors, exploring this Nordic gem can feel like deciphering ancient runes. This section will guide you through Oslo's layout with clear directions and a sprinkle of local flavor.

Orientation Essentials:

Oslo is conveniently divided into two main sections, East Oslo and West Oslo. The majestic Oslofjord acts as a natural divider, with its glistening waters carving through the heart of the city. The fjord is a Viking ship's keel, and the city unfolds on either side.

East Oslo:

- **Grünerløkka:** This trendy district oozes hipster charm and is packed with vintage shops, independent cafes, and buzzing nightlife. You'll encounter cobbled streets, colorful houses, and a palpable creative energy.

- **Vålerenga:** Formerly an industrial hub, Vålerenga has transformed into a hip haven for families and young professionals. Its waterfront promenade offers stunning fjord views, perfect for strolls.

- **Gamlebyen:** History buff alert. Gamlebyen, or Old Town, is Oslo's oldest district, boasting cobbled streets, wooden houses, and home to the Oslo viewpoint, where you can get captivating views of the city.

West Oslo:

- **Aker Brygge:** This former shipyard has morphed into a stylish waterfront district brimming with high-end boutiques, trendy restaurants, and lively bars. You'll find gleaming yachts bobbing in the harbor and the scent of fresh seafood tempting your taste buds.

- **Frogner:** Home to the iconic Vigeland Park, Frogner is a green oasis dotted with sculptures, perfect for picnics and leisurely walks. Don't miss the Monolitten, a giant granite obelisk, and the playful bronze statues that capture the essence of human life.

- **Majorstuen:** This upscale district pulsates with vibrant student energy. Boasting chic boutiques, trendy cafes, and a buzzing nightlife scene, Majorstuen is where Oslo's youth come to play.

Embracing the Fjord:

The Oslofjord is a geographical divider and the city's lifeblood. Whether hopping on a ferry to explore nearby islands, enjoying a scenic cruise at sunset, or simply sipping coffee at a waterfront cafe, the fjord adds a touch of magic to every experience.

Oslo's public transportation system is a dream come true. Trams glide through the streets, buses weave through neighborhoods, and the metro whisks you across the city in the blink of an eye. Invest in an Oslo Pass for unlimited travel and seamless exploration.

Remember, a map is just a starting point. Don't be afraid to get lost, stumble upon hidden delights, and soak in the local atmosphere. Chat with Osloites in cozy cafes, explore unexpected side streets, and discover the city's hidden wonders. Oslo awaits, ready to unfold its charm as a Viking saga comes to life.

Did You Know? Oslo's Winter Park transforms into a wonderland of towering ice sculptures every January. These intricate frozen artworks, created by international artists, are not just to admire but to climb, slide down, and explore.

From Viking Stronghold to Modern Marvel: Unraveling Oslo's Storied Past

Oslo pulsates with the energy of a modern metropolis. Yet, beneath its sleek skyscrapers and trendy cafes lies a history as rich and captivating as any Viking saga. Today, you journey through time, unraveling the myths that created Oslo, from its humble beginnings as a Viking stronghold to its transformation into a thriving modern capital.

Echoes of Vikings:

Oslo's story begins around 1048 AD, when Harald Hardrada, a fearsome Viking king, established a trading post on the banks of the Oslofjord. This modest settlement, initially named "Ánslo," quickly evolved into a strategic hub, drawing merchants and adventurers from across Scandinavia. One could find blacksmiths hammering axes, traders haggling over furs, and longships slicing through the fjord's icy waters.

A City Forged by Fire and Faith:

Oslo's early years were turbulent. Ravaged by fires and plagued by power struggles, the city persevered. In the 13th century, King Haakon V built Akershus Fortress, a formidable stone sentinel guarding the harbor. Later, Christianity took root, and St. Margaret's Church was built, a masterpiece of Gothic architecture, rose upon the hills. These landmarks are testaments to Oslo's resilience and its growing importance in the region.

A Plague of Change:

The Black Death swept through Europe in 1347, decimating Oslo's population and plunging the city into a period of stagnation. However, like the phoenix rising from ashes, Oslo gradually rebuilt itself. Trade flourished, and the city once again became a center of commerce and culture. The Renaissance brought a vibrant intellectual spirit, reflected in the establishment of Norway's first university in 1811.

Uniting a Nation:

In 1814, a pivotal moment arrived. Following centuries of Danish rule, Norway declared independence, and Oslo was chosen as the nation's capital. This newfound freedom sparked a period of rapid growth and transformation. Industries boomed, grand buildings like the Royal Palace arose, and Oslo stepped onto the world stage.

The 20th Century and Beyond:

The 20th century saw Oslo grapple with challenges and triumphs. World wars tested its resilience, while the discovery of oil in the North Sea brought prosperity and rapid modernization. Today, Oslo is a beacon of sustainability and innovation. Eco-friendly initiatives like car-free zones and clean energy projects make it a model for green cities worldwide.

A City of Contrasts:

Oslo's charm lies in its captivating contrasts. Modern skyscrapers stand tall alongside medieval fortresses, while trendy cafes hum with life in the shadow of ancient cathedrals. Vikings echo in the cobbled streets while the future gleams in the glass-and-steel facades. This juxtaposition of past and present is what makes Oslo genuinely unique.

Exploring Oslo's History:

Are you wondering how to experience Oslo's storied past firsthand? Explore the Viking Ship Museum, where ancient vessels whisper tales of seafaring adventures. Climb the ramparts of Akershus Fortress and imagine the clang of armor and the cries of battle. Stroll through the Gamlebyen, where time seems to slow down amidst wooden houses and cobbled lanes.

Oslo is more than just a modern capital with a fascinating past. Every corner tells a story, and every landmark speaks of resilience, cultural evolution, and the unwavering spirit of a nation. Come, wander through Oslo's streets, and let history unfold before your eyes.

Oslo's Gems: A Deeper Dive into the City's Treasures

Oslo radiates magnetic energy, drawing in travelers with its blend of historical grandeur, contemporary flair, and breathtaking natural beauty. This vibrant city is woven with must-visit attractions, each unveiling a unique facet of its identity. It's time to uncover some of these treasures, stirring your wanderlust and preparing you for an unforgettable Oslo escapade:

Aker Brygge: From a once-gritty shipyard, Aker Brygge has transformed into a waterfront haven of buzzing life. Sleek yachts bob gently in the fjord, trendy cafes entice with aromatic brews, and art galleries beckon with contemporary creations. Indulge in a seafood feast overlooking the water, explore the fascinating Astrup Fearnley Museum of Modern Art in nearby Tjuvholmen, or simply bask in the sun-kissed ambiance.

As of the writing of this book, you can visit Aker Brygge at any time during your visit. However, if you are planning on going shopping, the stores' normal opening hours are from Mondays to Fridays, from 10 am till 7 pm, and on Saturdays, from 10 am till 6 pm, but please always double-check the opening hours online should there have been any slight change in their schedule.

- **Significance:** This is a testament to Oslo's urban renewal and a vibrant leisure, dining, and art hub.

- **Unique Features:** Boat tours departing from the harbor, floating restaurants offering fjord views, and captivating street art adorning the buildings.

From a once-gritty shipyard, Aker Brygge has transformed into a waterfront haven of buzzing life.[7]

Holmenkollen: Beyond the city center, Holmenkollen comes with breathtaking views and exhilarating experiences. Ascend the iconic Holmenkollen Ski Jump, one of the world's largest, and imagine the thrill of soaring down its slopes. Explore the fascinating Holmenkollen Ski Museum, delving into the history of Norway's national sport. For a gentler pace, hike through the lush Nordmarka forest, breathing in the crisp Nordic air and soaking in the serene beauty.

As of the writing of this book, the normal opening hours for the Ski Museum and the Jump Tower are from Mondays to Wednesdays and from Fridays to Sundays, from 10 am till 5 pm, and on Thursdays, from 10 am till 8 pm, but please always double-check the opening hours online should there have been any slight change in their schedule.

- **Significance:** A haven for sports enthusiasts and nature lovers, offering stunning panoramas and a taste of Oslo's outdoor spirit.
- **Unique Features:** Experience the adrenaline rush of the ski jump simulator, visit the interactive Viking village, and take in breathtaking views from the observation deck.

Ascend the iconic Holmenkollen Ski Jump, one of the world's largest, and imagine the thrill of soaring down its slopes.[8]

The National Museum: Art lovers, rejoice! The National Museum is a treasure trove of Norwegian and international art, spanning centuries and styles. From Edvard Munch's emotive masterpieces to captivating works by J.C. Dahl and Christian Krohg, prepare to be mesmerized by the sheer artistic talent on display. Wander through the grand halls, admire the intricate decorative art collection, and lose yourself in the world of creativity.

As of the writing of this book, the normal opening hours are from Thursdays to Sundays, from 10 am till 5 pm, closed on Mondays, and on Tuesdays and Wednesdays, from 10 am till 8 pm, but please always double-check the opening hours online should there have been any slight change in their schedule.

- **Significance:** Housing Norway's most significant art collection offers a comprehensive journey through the country's artistic heritage.

- **Unique Features:** Rotational exhibitions featuring international artists, interactive displays for children, and breathtaking views of the Royal Palace gardens from the rooftop terrace.

The National Museum is a treasure trove of Norwegian and international art, spanning centuries and styles.[9]

Frogner Park: Step into a green oasis amidst the urban bustle at Frogner Park. Lush gardens, tranquil ponds, and winding paths invite strolls and peaceful moments. Discover the captivating world of Gustav Vigeland's sculptures, from the playful children's playground to the iconic Monolitten, a towering granite obelisk piercing the sky. Picnic under the shade of majestic trees, enjoy a coffee at a café and experience the serene side of Oslo.

As of the writing of this book, the normal opening hours daily are all 24 hours of the day, but please always double-check the opening hours online should there have been any slight change in their schedule.

- **Significance:** A haven of tranquility and artistic expression, offering a delightful escape from the city's energy.

- **Unique Features:** Guided sculpture tours, hidden nooks and crannies to explore, and seasonal events like open-air concerts and Christmas markets.

Step into a green oasis amidst the urban bustle at Frogner Park.[10]

The Fram Museum: Embark on an Arctic adventure without leaving Oslo at the Fram Museum. Witness the legendary polar ship Fram, which conquered the North and South Poles, and be transported to the frozen landscapes it braved. Learn about the intrepid explorers who ventured into the unknown, experience life aboard the ship through interactive exhibits, and marvel at the resilience of both man and machinery.

As of the writing of this book, the normal opening hours are daily, from 9:30 am till 6 pm, but please always double-check the opening hours online should there have been any slight change in their schedule.

- **Significance:** Offers a fascinating glimpse into polar exploration and the history of maritime travel.

- **Unique Features:** Explore the Fram's cramped quarters, climb the mast for panoramic views, and watch a captivating film about the ship's voyages.

Embark on an Arctic adventure without leaving Oslo at the Fram Museum.[11]

Expanding Your Horizons:

- **Bygdøy Peninsula:** This historical hub boasts several treasures beyond the Fram Museum. Uncover Viking lore at the Viking Ship Museum, where ancient vessels foretell tales of seafaring adventures. Explore maritime history at the Kon-Tiki Museum, marveling at Thor Heyerdahl's daring raft voyages. Get a glimpse of Norwegian cultural heritage at the Norwegian Folk Museum, with its traditional buildings and fascinating exhibits.

- **Frogner:** While Frogner Park and Vigeland sculptures are must-sees, don't miss the Astrup Fearnley Museum of Modern Art. Housing an impressive collection of contemporary art, from Munch to Picasso, it offers a captivating counterpoint to the classical sculptures outside.

- **Sofienberg:** This trendy neighborhood, just north of the Royal Palace, offers a glimpse into Oslo's bohemian spirit.

This is just a taste of the many treasures waiting to be unearthed in Oslo. Whether you're drawn to history, art, nature, or all of the above, this city has something to ignite your passions and leave you with an unforgettable Nordic experience.

Did You Know? The iconic Oslo Opera House, with its sloping rooftop resembling a glacier melting into the fjord, doubles as a giant climbing wall in the summer. Strap on your harness and ascend the white granite slopes for breathtaking city views and bragging rights.

Oslo's Vibrant Experiences: Where Culture and Cuisine Collide

Oslo's heartbeat is as much artistic as it is urban. This vibrant city isn't just a collection of buildings. It's a living, breathing canvas where culture, music, and literature intertwine with a delectable culinary scene, creating an exhilarating and soul-stirring experience.

A City Steeped in the Arts:

Oslo's appreciation for the arts is evident in every corner. From the iconic Opera House, a breathtaking architectural masterpiece that rises from the fjord like a sculpted wave, to the majestic National Museum housing centuries of artistic treasures, the city is a haven for art lovers. Immerse yourself in Munch's emotive masterpieces, be captivated by Vigeland's sculptures in Frogner Park, or discover contemporary creations in the cutting-edge Astrup Fearnley Museum.

Melodies that Move the Soul:

Oslo's musical landscape is as diverse as its people. From the hauntingly beautiful melodies of traditional folk music to the electrifying energy of contemporary electronica, the city's stages pulsate with rhythm. Catch a concert at the iconic Oslo Concert Hall, where world-renowned orchestras perform under the shimmering crystal chandelier, or lose yourself in the intimate atmosphere of a cozy jazz bar.

Pages that Unfold Worlds:

Oslo is a city where literature whispers from the cobbled streets. Dive into the captivating narratives of Nobel Prize laureates at the Nobel Peace Center, explore the vibrant literary scene at independent bookstores, or attend poetry readings at atmospheric cafes. Let the words of Ibsen and Bjørnson transport you to another time and discover the rich allure of Norwegian storytelling.

Celebrating Life's Rhythms:

Oslo's cultural calendar is a kaleidoscope of vibrant festivals and celebrations. Immerse yourself in the revelry of the Constitution Day parade, where children in traditional *bunads* dance through the streets. Witness the mesmerizing spectacle of the Oslo Opera Festival, where international artists grace the stage with their musical brilliance. For a taste of local tradition, join the Christmas markets, where the air is filled with the aroma of gløgg and the warmth of the community.

A Culinary Adventure for the Senses:

Oslo's culinary scene is a delectable blend of tradition and innovation. Indulge in the simplicity of fresh seafood plucked straight from the fjord at Mathallen food hall, or savor contemporary Nordic cuisine at Michelin-starred restaurants like Maaemo. Try traditional dishes like fårikål (stewed lamb and cabbage) or brunost (brown cheese) at cozy neighborhood restaurants for a taste of history. And don't forget to explore Oslo's vibrant street food scene, where food trucks and stalls offer everything from savory sausages to melt-in-your-mouth pastries.

Where to Experience Oslo's Culinary Magic:

- **For Fine Dining with Nordic Flair:** Maaemo, Kontrast.

   Maaemo Address: Dronning Eufemias gate 23, 0194 Oslo, Norway.

   Kontrast Address: Maridalsveien 15a, 0175 Oslo, Norway.

- **For Traditional Norwegian Fare:** Statholdergaarden, Olympen.

   Statholdergaarden Address: Radhusgata 11, 0151 Oslo, Norway.

   Olympen Address: Gronlandsleiret, 0190 Oslo, Norway.

- **For a Taste of the Fjord:** Fiskeriet, Aker Brygge, SALT Art and Music.

   Fiskeriet Address: Youngstorget 2b, 0181 Oslo, Norway.

   Aker Brygge Address: Aker Brygge, Oslo, Norway.

   SALT Art and Music Address: Langkaia 1, 0150 Oslo, Norway.

- **For Street Food Adventures:** Torggata Botaniske, Youngstorget, Løkka Food Court.

   Torggata Botaniske Address: Torggata 17B, 0183 Oslo, Norway.

   Youngstorget Address: Youngstorget, 0181 Oslo, Norway.

   Løkka Food Court Address: Thorvald Meyers gate 68, 0552 Oslo, Norway.

Oslo is a city that invites you to savor every moment. Let yourself be swept away by the rhythm of its music, lose yourself in the pages of its stories, and indulge in the delectable culinary scene. This vibrant Nordic capital is waiting to unfold its magic, one experience at a time.

Did You Know? Oslo is also a bookworm's paradise. Dive into independent cafes filled with bibliophiles, explore second-hand shops overflowing with treasures, and discover the next page-turner amidst the literary buzz.

Shopping, Sleep, and Getting Around

Oslo's allure extends far beyond its stunning scenery. Whether you're a fashionista on the hunt for one-of-a-kind finds, a budget traveler seeking cozy digs, or a road trip enthusiast exploring Norway by car, this vibrant city has something for everyone. Are you ready to dive into the details:

Shopping Spree:

Aker Brygge: This waterfront haven of sleek yachts and trendy cafes is also a shopper's paradise. Luxurious designer boutiques like Chanel and Gucci rub shoulders with contemporary Norwegian brands like Holzweiler and Samsøe Samsøe. Don't miss the Aker Brygge Shopping Center for a mix of high-street fashion and everyday essentials.

Grünerløkka: Step into the hipster haven of Grünerløkka, where vintage clothing stores like Fretex and quirky shops like Manillusion offer a treasure trove of unique finds. Explore independent record stores, browse antique markets, and discover local design gems.

Slumber for Every Dream:

Luxury and Uniqueness: Treat yourself to the opulent grandeur of The Thief, where minimalist Nordic design meets breathtaking fjord views. For a touch of historical charm, The Grand Hotel offers a glimpse into Oslo's aristocratic past. And for a truly unique experience, check out the Amerikalinjen, a converted cruise ship docked by the Opera House.

The Thief Address: Landgangen 1, 0252 Oslo, Norway.

The Grand Hotel Address: Karl Johans gt. 31, 0159 Oslo, Norway.

Amerikalinjen Address: Jernbanetorget 2, 0154 Oslo, Norway.

Budget-Friendly and Local: Cozy up in a guesthouse like the Guesthouse Center Oslo City or Anker Hostel, perfect for meeting fellow travelers. Opt for a vacation rental in vibrant neighborhoods like Majorstuen or Frogner for a taste of local life.

Guesthouse Center Oslo City Address: Breigata 19, 0187 Oslo, Norway.

Anker Hostel Address: Storgata 53H, 0182 Oslo, Norway.

Finding Your Base Camp:

Central City: Immerse yourself in the heart of the action by staying near Karl Johans gate, the main shopping street. You'll have easy access to sights, public transportation, and buzzing nightlife.

Grünerløkka: Experience the hipster pulse and independent shops firsthand. This bohemian neighborhood offers a vibrant atmosphere and trendy cafes.

Bygdøy Peninsula: Nestled amidst museums and historical sites, Bygdøy offers peace with stunning fjord views. Perfect for escaping the city's bustle.

Navigating the City:

- **Public Transportation:** Oslo's efficient transport network makes getting around a breeze. Invest in an Oslo Pass for unlimited travel and skip the ticket queues.

- **Taxis and Ride-Sharing:** Taxis are readily available, especially near major attractions and hotels. Uber and other ride-sharing services are also popular options.

- **Car Travel:** Oslo is driving-friendly, with well-maintained roads and designated parking areas. Keep in mind that tolls are common, and central parking can be expensive. Distances by car: Aker Brygge is 1.5 miles from the city center, while Grünerløkka is 2 miles away.

Bonus Tip: Explore Oslo on two wheels. Rent a bike and cycle through the city's dedicated bike lanes for a healthy and sustainable way to see the sights.

Oslo is a city that caters to every budget, taste, and travel style. With its vibrant shopping scene, diverse accommodation options, and efficient transportation system, Oslo is waiting to be explored, one fjord, one street, and one delicious street food bite at a time.

Did You now? Edvard Munch, the renowned artist behind "The Scream," spent his formative years in Oslo. Explore his former home, now a museum, and delve into the city's influence on his haunting yet captivating works. You might even hear echoes of Viking angst in his brushstrokes.

Oslo's Day Trip Delights and Local Gems

Oslo's charm extends far beyond its captivating streets. To enrich your Nordic adventure, consider these inspiring day trips and local experiences:

Escape to the Fjords:

Bygdøy Peninsula: Sail across the sparkling Oslofjord to Bygdøy, a museum haven (Viking Ship Museum, Fram Museum) and historical treasure (Norwegian Folkemuseum). Explore the captivating Vigeland Park and enjoy a picnic amidst its iconic sculptures.

Drøbak: Take a scenic train ride to this coastal town. Stroll along the harbor, admire the iconic Oscarsborg Fortress, and indulge in fresh seafood at a waterfront restaurant.

Art and Culture Beyond the City Center:

Kistefos Museum and Sculpture Park: Escape to this architectural gem just outside Oslo. Gaze in wonder at modern art exhibits and stroll through the whimsical sculpture park, all nestled amidst rolling hills and serene natural beauty.

Local Customs and Etiquette:

- **Greeting:** A firm handshake and direct eye contact are customary.
- **Personal Space:** Norwegians value personal space, so maintain a comfortable distance during conversations.
- **Tipping:** Tipping is not expected, but a small gratuity for exceptional service is appreciated.
- **Punctuality:** Norwegians are known for their punctuality, so they arrive on time for appointments and meetings.

Entertainment and Nightlife:

Blå: Immerse yourself in this legendary jazz club's vibrant live music scene, featuring both local and international artists.

Address: Brenneriveien 9C, 0182 Oslo, Norway.

Oslo Pride: Celebrate diversity and inclusivity at this annual festival, filled with parades, concerts, and cultural events. (Dates vary, typically in June)

Bonus Tip: Learn a few basic Norwegian phrases! "Hei" (hi), "Takk" (thank you), and "Vennligst" (please) go a long way in showing your respect and appreciation for the local culture.

Did You Know? Oslo proudly hosts the Nobel Peace Prize ceremony in the grand City Hall every December. Witness history unfolding in this elegant venue, soak in the festive atmosphere, and ponder the values of peace and hope that Oslo holds dear.

As you bid farewell to Oslo, leaving behind its vibrant streets and captivating art, remember that this city isn't just a collection of sights and sounds. It's a kaleidoscope of experiences that will linger in your memory long after your flight departs. Oslo whispers tales of Viking kings and Edvard Munch's brushstrokes. It dances to the rhythm of contemporary life and feeds your soul with steaming bowls of fish soup and sleek architectural wonders.

Carry a piece of its magic with you, whether it's a hand-knitted sweater adorned with Viking runes, a photograph capturing the sunset over the fjord, or simply the echoes of laughter shared with newfound friends. Oslo has embraced you, and now it's your turn to carry its spirit with you, reminding you that the magic of Norway always awaits, just beyond the next adventure.

Chapter 4: Eastern Norway (Østlandet)

Eastern Norway (Østlandet), the beating heart of Scandinavia, pulsates with vibrant energy and endless possibilities. This expansive region, home to the captivating capital of Oslo, is a mosaic of diverse landscapes, rich history, and captivating experiences. Families will find enchanting amusement parks and historic towns, while adventure seekers can conquer mountain peaks, navigate rushing rivers, and explore hidden forests. Nature lovers, meanwhile, will find solace in

Østlandet.[12]

the embrace of tranquil fjords, majestic valleys, and sprawling national parks.

Hold on, adventurer. A recent twist in the map has unfolded. In 2020, some county borders were redrawn, merging familiar names into exciting new entities. So, be prepared for surprises as you navigate this evolving

---

landscape, ensuring you have the most updated information to unlock the magic of Eastern Norway.

Unveiling Vestfold og Telemark: Where History Whispers and Nature Roars

Nestled along Norway's southern coast, Vestfold og Telemark beckons with a captivating duality. Here, two distinct and proud regions, the former counties of Telemark and Vestfold, have come together to form history, adventure, and breathtaking beauty.

Historical Background

Telemark, steeped in Viking lore and boasting the title of Norway's "ski cradle," echoed with the clang of hammers shaping longships and the rhythmic chants of saga tellers. Vestfold, meanwhile, emerged as a center of trade and power, with Tønsberg, Norway's oldest city, serving as a vibrant hub long before the Viking Age. Today, this rich heritage lives on in ancient burial mounds, soaring cathedrals, and the very names of towns whispered across centuries.

Did You Know? In Telemark, the Telemark Canal, a marvel of engineering, snakes through 105 kilometers of locks and aqueducts, offering a taste of Norway's industrial past and breathtaking scenery.

Main Attractions

Tønsberg: Explore the ancient streets of Norway's oldest city, marvel at the Tønsberg Cathedral, delve into Viking history at the Haugar Art Museum, and soak in the coastal panoramas.

Explore the ancient streets of Norway's oldest city and delve into Viking history at the Haugar Art Museum.[13]

Larvik: Discover Viking burial mounds of the 7th-century "Queen Asa," and relax on the pristine beaches of Farris Bad.

Skien: Cruise through the scenic Telemark Canal, and visit the Ibsen Museum dedicated to Norway's renowned playwright.

As of the writing of this book, the normal opening hours daily are all 24 hours of the day, but please always double-check the opening hours online should there have been any slight change in their schedule.

Cruise through the scenic Telemark Canal.[14]

Rjukan: Ascend Mount Gaustatoppen, Scandinavia's southernmost peak, explore the industrial heritage of the Vemork power plant and wonder at the architectural marvel of Rjukan church.

As of the writing of this book, the normal opening hours daily are all 24 hours of the day, but please always double-check the opening hours online should there have been any slight change in their schedule.

The architectural marvel of the Rjukan church will amaze you.[15]

Heddal Stave Church: Travel back in time at the iconic Heddal Stave Church, a UNESCO World Heritage Site, and admire its intricate craftsmanship and captivating history.

As of the writing of this book, the attraction is temporarily closed, but please always double-check the opening hours online should there have been any slight change in their schedule.

Admire the Heddal Stave Church's intricate craftsmanship and captivating history.[16]

Transport:

Vestfold og Telemark is easily accessible by plane (Oslo Airport Gardermoen), train (national rail network), and car (well-maintained roads). Ferry services operate across the Oslofjord.

Experiences:

Viking Voyage: Sail the Oslofjord aboard a replica Viking ship, feel the wind in your hair, and experience life as a Norse voyager.

Telemark Canal Cruise: Embark on a leisurely journey through the Telemark Canal, soak in the verdant landscapes, and witness the engineering marvel unfold.

Gaustatoppen Hike: Conquer the majestic Mount Gaustatoppen, Norway's southernmost peak, and be rewarded with stunning panoramic views.

Heddal Stave Church Concert: Immerse yourself in the haunting tones of a traditional concert within the walls of the historic Heddal Stave Church.

Larvik Fjord Kayaking: Paddle through the serene waters of the Larvik Fjord, marvel at the coastal beauty, and spot the playful seals.

Did You Know? Tønsberg in Vestfold boasts the Haugar Art Museum, home to the Viking Ship Museum, where majestic wooden vessels slumber, frozen in time.

Family Fun:

Bø Sommarland: Plunge into the watery thrills of Bø Sommarland, the largest water park in Norway, featuring slides, pools, and endless aquatic adventures.

Address: Steintjonnvegen 2, 3800 Bø I Telemark, Norway.

Telemark Canal Boat Tour: Embark on a family-friendly canal cruise, spot fascinating wildlife, and learn about the canal's rich history.

Akersvannet Nature Reserve: Explore the trails and boardwalks of Akersvannet, a scenic nature reserve perfect for family hikes, picnics, and wildlife spotting.

Address: Akersvannet, 3173 Stokke, Norway.

Gullkronene Sculpture Park: Wander through the colorful open-air art gallery of Gullkronene, let your imagination run wild amidst the sculptures, and enjoy the panoramic views.

Address: 3170 Sem, Norway

Where to Eat:

Kokeriet Restaurant: Savor fresh seafood and local delicacies with stunning harbor views at this waterfront restaurant.

Address: Brygga 1, 3210 Sandefjord, Norway.

Andre Etasje: Experience fine dining with breathtaking panoramic views at this beautiful restaurant.

Address: Nedre Lannggate 49, 3126 Tonsberg, Norway.

Himalaya Tandori: Embark on a wonderful Indian dining experience in this amazing restaurant, where even the service is highly praised.

Address: Strandpromenaden 9, 3187 Horten, Norway.

Shopping Guide:

AMFI Larvik: Browse through a mix of international brands and local stores in this modern shopping center.

Address: Jegersborggata 4, 3256 Larvik, Norway.

Bøsenteret: Find everything from sporting goods and homeware to fashion and electronics at this convenient shopping park near Bø Sommarland.

Address: Stasjonsvegen 28, 3800 Bø I Telemark, Norway.

Arkkaden Skien: Right in the middle of the city center, Arkkaden Skien offers a wide variety of stores and restaurants. Arkkaden follows the motto "everything for the city" and has been part of the activities that led to a folk festival in Skien.

Address: Bruene 1, 3724 Skien, Norway.

Entertainment:

Teater Ibsen in Skien: Immerse yourself in the world of renowned playwright Henrik Ibsen at this iconic theater, showcasing modern interpretations of his classic works.

Address: Hollendrigata 15, 3732 Skien, Norway.

Larvik Guitar Festival: Join the vibrant festivities of the Larvik Guitar Festival, featuring concerts, workshops, and gear expos.

Tønsberg Christmas Market: Join the festive spirit at the Tønsberg Christmas Market, brimming with twinkling lights, handmade decorations, and heartwarming delicacies.

Sports and Leisure:

Hiking and Skiing: Lace up your boots and explore the diverse landscapes of Vestfold og Telemark, from serene forest trails to challenging mountain hikes. In winter, hit the slopes at renowned ski resorts like Gaustatoppen or Norefjell.

Kayaking and Fishing: Paddle through the calm waters of fjords and lakes, or cast your line and soak in the tranquility of nature. Guided tours and rentals are available.

Golfing: Swing your clubs at one of the picturesque golf courses in the region, offering stunning fjord views and challenging rounds.

Cycling: Embark on scenic bike rides along dedicated cycling paths, explore villages, and enjoy the fresh air.

Rock Climbing: Scale the rocky cliffs and experience the thrill of outdoor climbing in challenging areas like Rjukan.

Accommodations:

Luxury Hotels: Indulge in five-star comfort at hotels like Farris Bad in Larvik or Dalen Hotel in Telemark, offering spa treatments, gourmet dining, and breathtaking views.

Farris Bad Address: Fritzo Brygge 2, 3264 Larvik, Norway.

Dalen Hotel Address: Hotellvegen 33, 3880 Dalen, Norway

Cozy Cabins: Rent a traditional Norwegian cabin nestled amidst the forests or by the fjord, perfect for a relaxing getaway.

Charming Bed and Breakfasts: Experience local hospitality and personalized service at bed and breakfasts across the region.

Campsites and Cottages: Pitch your tent or rent a cozy cottage for a budget-friendly and adventurous stay in nature.

Boutique Hotels: Discover stylish boutique hotels in major towns like Tønsberg and Skien, offering a memorable and personalized experience.

Vestfold og Telemark is a destination for all seasons, offering something for every traveler. Summer brings warm days, long hours of daylight, and vibrant festivals. Autumn paints the landscape in vibrant hues, perfect for hiking and exploring. Winter transforms the region into a snowy wonderland, ideal for winter sports and cozy evenings by the fireplace. Spring awakens the region with fresh blooms and verdant landscapes, perfect for nature lovers.

Unveiling Viken: Where History Echoes and Landscapes Beckon

Viken, nestled amidst the verdant embrace of Eastern Norway, is formed from the threads of three proud former counties, including Akershus, Buskerud, and Østfold. Born in 2020 from their union, Viken pulsates with history, stuns with its diverse landscapes, and beckons explorers with its unique blend of urban buzz and rural charm.

Historical Background:

Each part of Viken reminds you of tales of the past. Akershus, guarding the majestic Oslofjord, bears the scars of Viking raids and sagas of medieval castles. Buskerud, cradled by snow-capped mountains, echoes with the clang of hammers in Kongsberg's legendary silver mines and the rhythmic tread of skiers conquering legendary Holmenkollen. Østfold, a land of rolling farmlands and vibrant coastal towns, holds Viking burial mounds and the legacy of industrial pioneers. Today, these rich heritages intertwine, creating a region where ancient whispers mingle with modern rhythms.

Main Attractions:

Kongsberg Silver Mines (UNESCO World Heritage Site): Explore the labyrinthine tunnels and discover the fascinating history of Norway's largest silver mine at the Norwegian Mining Museum.

As of the writing of this book, the opening hours for the museum are from Tuesday to Sunday from 12 pm to 4 pm and closed on Monday, but please always double-check the opening hours online should there have been any slight change in their schedule.

Explore the labyrinthine tunnels and discover the fascinating history of Norway's largest silver mine.[17]

Oslofjord Islands: Escape the city's bustle and sail to car-free islands like Lindøya and Hovedøya, where quiet beaches, historical fortifications, and scenic hiking trails await.

As of the writing of this book, the normal opening hours daily are all 24 hours of the day, but please always double-check the opening hours online should there have been any slight change in their schedule.

Escape the city's bustle and sail to car-free islands.[18]

Drammen Canal: Cruise along the Drammen Canal, a marvel of engineering connecting the Oslofjord to Drammen, and admire the city's vibrant waterfront from a serene perspective.

As of the writing of this book, the normal opening hours daily are all 24 hours of the day, but please always double-check the opening hours online should there have been any slight change in their schedule.

Cruise along the Drammen Canal, a marvel of engineering connecting the Oslofjord to Drammen[19]

Fredrikstad Fortress: Step back in time at this impressive 17th-century fortress, the largest preserved in Northern Europe, and delve into its military history.

The fortress area is open every day all year, day and night, but please always double-check the opening hours online should there have been any slight change in their schedule.

Step back in time to this impressive 17th-century fortress, the largest preserved in Northern Europe, and delve into its military history.[20]

Transport:

Viken is easy to navigate by train, bus, and car. Public transportation within Oslo and major cities is efficient and affordable. Intercity travel is well-connected by trains and buses, and several national roads crisscross the region. Ferry services operate on the Oslofjord and offer fascinating travel experiences.

Experiences:

Viking Ship Cruise: Sail the Oslofjord aboard a replica Viking ship, feel the wind in your hair, and immerse yourself in the world of these legendary seafarers.

Drammen River Walk: Follow the idyllic Drammenselva River through lush forests and neighborhoods, discovering hidden waterfalls and enjoying tranquil scenery.

Nesbyen Horseback Riding: Saddle up and explore the scenic valleys and forests of Nesbyen on horseback, experiencing the region's unique rural charm.

Fredrikstad Ghost Walk: Uncover the chilling history of Fredrikstad with a guided ghost walk through the dark alleys and spooky corners of the historic town.

Lillestrøm Ice Hockey Game: Cheer on the local team, Lørenskog IK, at a thrilling ice hockey game and experience the electrifying atmosphere of Norwegian sports.

Family Fun:

TusenFryd Amusement Park: Let loose at Norway's largest amusement park, which has an adrenaline-pumping mix of rollercoasters, water rides, and family-friendly shows.

Address: Fryds Vei 25, 1407 Vinterbro, Norway.

Akershus Fortress: Explore the historic Akershus Fortress, with its dungeons, cannons, and museums, and let your imagination run wild with tales of knights and princesses.

Address: 0150 Oslo, Norway.

Drammen Aquatics Center: Take a refreshing dip in the pools and slides of Drammen Aquatics Center, offering fun for all ages and a welcome escape on a hot summer day.

Address: Danvikgata 40, 3045 Drammen, Norway.

Did You Know? Renowned composer Edvard Grieg found inspiration in Viken's landscapes, and his melodies still echo through the valleys and forests.

Where to Eat:

Alpenhaus Drammen: Savor local delicacies at Alpenhaus Restaurant with a pleasant atmosphere.

Address: Tollbugata 12B, 3044 Drammen, Norway.

The Bear House in Nesbyen: Experience fresh baked goods and coffee daily at The Bear House. In the evening, they also serve Napolian-style pizza, serving high-quality dishes with authentic ingredients.

Address: Jordeshagen 3, 3540 Nesbyen, Norway.

Mirabel Restaurant and Bar in Lillestrøm: Located in the center of the city, Mirabel Restaurant and Bar offers a variety of food from different cuisines. The restaurant also offers a comfortable atmosphere.

Shopping Guide:

Osloveien in Oslo: Explore the chic boutiques and designer stores lining Osloveien, a haven for fashionistas seeking high-end clothing, accessories, and homeware.

Address: Osloveien, Ringerike, Norway.

Magasinet Drammen Shopping Center: Discover unique finds and local crafts at Magasinet, a marketplace housed in a historic building featuring independent shops, galleries, and cafes.

Address: Nedre Storgate 6, 30115 Drammen, Norway.

Fredrikstad Gamlebyen: Wander through the cobblestone streets of Fredrikstad Gamle By, lined with antique shops, art galleries, and independent boutiques, offering a treasure trove of unique finds.

Address: Gamlebyen, 1632 Fredrikstad, Norway.

Lillestrøm Outlets: Score deals on designer brands and popular clothing at outlets in Lillestrøm, the perfect destination for bargain hunters and fashion enthusiasts.

Entertainment:

Oslo Opera House: Visit a sublime opera or ballet performance at the iconic Oslo Opera House, a stunning architectural masterpiece overlooking the Oslofjord.

Address: Kirsten Flagstads Plass 1, 0150 Oslo, Norway.

Drammen Theater: Enjoy a diverse range of productions, from classic dramas to contemporary comedies, at the historic Drammen Theater, a cultural hub in the heart of the city.

Address: Ovre Storgate 12, 3018 Drammen, Norway.

Fredrikstad Fredriksten Festival: Immerse yourself in medieval history at the Fredriksten Festival, with jousting tournaments, historical reenactments, and live music within the walls of the fortress.

Sports and Leisure:

Holmenkollen Ski Jump: Conquer the iconic Holmenkollen ski jump, a legendary venue for winter sports enthusiasts, and admire breathtaking panoramic views of Oslo.

Tyrifjorden: Explore the vast Tyrifjorden, Norway's fifth-largest lake, by kayak, sailboat, or stand-up paddleboard, and enjoy the serene beauty of the surrounding landscapes.

Hallingskarvet National Park: Hike through the breathtaking landscapes of Hallingdal National Park, encountering towering mountains, pristine lakes, and diverse wildlife.

Address: Rallarvegen 2660, 5179 Finse, Norwat.

Fredrikstad Golf Club: Tee off on the scenic Fredrikstad Golf Club, a challenging course with stunning fjord views, perfect for golfers of all skill levels.

Address: Torsnesveien 16, 1630 Gamle Fredrikstad, Norway.

Accommodations:

Luxury: The Clarion Collection Hotel Tollboden boasts stunning fjord views and a rooftop bar with panoramic city vistas. For a unique experience, consider staying in the converted industrial building of Comfort Hotel Union Brygge, which offers modern apartments and an on-site brewery.

Clarion Collection Hotel Tollboden Address: Tollbugata 43, 3044 Drammen, Norway.

Comfort Hotel Union Brygge Address: Gronland 64, 3045 Drammen, Norway.

Mid-Range: The Thon Hotel Lillestrøm, connected to the Thon Arena, is perfect for sports enthusiasts. Alternatively, consider the Scandic Lillestrøm, conveniently located near the train station and shopping center.

Thon Hotel Lillestrøm Address: Storgata 25, 2001 Lillestrøm, Norway

Scandic Lillestrøm: Stillverksveien 28, 2004, Lillestrøm, Norway.

Budget: Anker Hostel, housed in a converted brewery, boasts a vibrant atmosphere and social events. For a unique experience, consider the P-Hotels, which has relaxed rooms with many complimentary facilities. .

Anker Hostel Address: Storgata 53H, 0182 Oslo, Norway.

P-Hotel Oslo Address: Grensen 19, 0159 Oslo, Norway.

Consider searching for unusual Airbnb stays in historic farmhouses, bed and breakfasts in quaint villages, or cozy cabins tucked away in the forests. Viken offers a kaleidoscope of lodging options, so choose the one that resonates with your travel style and budget to create your perfect Viken experience.

Innlandet: Where Mountains Whisper and Lakes Shimmer

In the heart of Norway lies Innlandet. It's a land cradled by towering peaks, kissed by shimmering lakes, and etched with the tales of Viking sagas and Olympic triumphs. Born from the union of Oppland and

Hedmark in 2020, Innlandet is a breathtaking canvas of rugged wilderness, villages, and vibrant cultural heritage, beckoning explorers of all kinds.

Historical Background:

Vikings carved their legends into the Innlandet landscape, leaving behind burial mounds and runestones telling of ancient battles and daring voyages. Medieval trade routes pulsed through valleys, connecting villages and fostering rich traditions. In the 19th century, the timber industry blossomed, leaving its mark on towns and shaping the region's character. Today, Innlandet embraces its diverse past, offering modern cities alongside historical treasures, where centuries whisper in the rustling leaves and ancient folklore dances in the wind.

Main Attractions:

Lillehammer Olympic Park: Relive the 1994 Winter Olympics at this iconic park, boasting ski jumps, bobsled tracks, and ice hockey rinks. Take a breathtaking chairlift ride for panoramic views, or try your hand at luge or bobsleigh experiences.

As of the writing of this book, the normal opening hours are every day from 9 am to 7 pm, but please always double-check the opening hours online should there have been any slight change in their schedule.

Relive the 1994 Winter Olympics at this iconic park, boasting ski jumps, bobsled tracks, and ice hockey rinks.[21]

Maihaugen Open-Air Museum: Step back in time at Maihaugen, Norway's largest open-air museum. Explore farmhouses, traditional workshops, and historical exhibits, bringing the rural life of days gone by to life.

As of the writing of this book, the normal opening hours are every day from 10 am to 5 pm, but please always double-check the opening hours online should there have been any slight change in their schedule.

Step back in time at Maihaugen, Norway's largest open-air museum.[22]

Jotunheimen National Park: Embark on an epic adventure in Jotunheimen, a wonderland of snow-capped peaks, shimmering glaciers, and pristine valleys. Hike through alpine meadows, conquer challenging trails, and marvel at the majesty of nature.

As of the writing of this book, the normal opening hours are daily all 24 hours of the day, but please always double-check the opening hours online should there have been any slight change in their schedule.

Embark on an epic adventure in Jotunheimen, a wonderland of snow-capped peaks, shimmering glaciers, and pristine valleys.[23]

Rondane National Park: Discover a gentler side of nature in Rondane, famed for its rolling mountains, verdant valleys, and abundant wildlife. Hike amidst wild reindeer herds, explore glacial lakes, and enjoy the tranquility of this majestic wilderness.

As of the writing of this book, the normal opening hours daily are all 24 hours of the day, but please always double-check the opening hours online should there have been any slight change in their schedule.

Discover a gentler side of nature in Rondane, famed for its rolling mountains, verdant valleys, and abundant wildlife.[24]

Lake Mjøsa: Cruise along the shores of Lake Mjøsa, Norway's largest lake, soaking in the captivating scenery. Visit waterfront towns, rent a kayak or sailboat, or enjoy a dip in the crystal-clear waters.

As of the writing of this book, the normal opening hours daily are all 24 hours of the day, but please always double-check the opening hours online should there have been any slight change in their schedule.

Cruise along the shores of Lake Mjøsa, Norway's largest lake, soaking in the captivating scenery.[25]

Transport:

Innlandet is easily accessible by train, bus, and car. Public transportation within major cities like Lillehammer and Hamar is efficient and affordable. Intercity travel is well-connected by trains and buses, and several national roads crisscross the region. Ferry services operate on Lake Mjøsa, offering unique travel experiences.

Experiences:

Viking Ship Cruise: Sail the waters of Lake Mjøsa aboard a replica Viking ship, feeling the wind in your hair and immersing yourself in the world of these legendary voyagers.

Gudbrandsdalen Bygdetun Tour: Travel back in time on a guided tour of Gudbrandsdalen Bygdetun, an open-air museum showcasing traditional farmhouses, workshops, and historical exhibits. Learn about local crafts, farming practices, and the valley's rich heritage.

Rondane Musk Ox Safari: Embark on an unusual adventure on a musk ox safari in Rondane National Park. Once extinct in Norway, these majestic creatures have been reintroduced and now roam the wild landscapes, offering a rare and exciting encounter.

Lillehammer Christmas Market: Immerse yourself in the festive spirit during the Lillehammer Christmas Market, held annually in December. Stroll through stalls adorned with twinkling lights, savor traditional treats, and soak in the magical atmosphere.

Galdhøpiggen Peak Summit Hike: Conquer the highest peak in Norway on a guided hike to Galdhøpiggen's summit. This challenging journey rewards seasoned adventurers with breathtaking panoramas and a sense of accomplishment.

Family Fun:

Hunderfossen Family Park: Let loose at Hunderfossen Family Park, featuring thrilling rollercoasters, water rides, and live shows for all ages. Enjoy a day of laughter, screams, and family fun in this magical amusement park.

Address: Fossekrovegen 22, 2625 Faberg, Norway.

Jorekstad Waterpark: Splash, slide, and play at Jorekstad Waterpark, offering hours of aquatic fun for the whole family. You can even spend the night at one of their comfortable cabins with modern facilities.

Address: Jorstadmovegen 690, 2625 Faberg, Norway.

Norwegian Railway Museum: Take a journey through time at the Norwegian Railway Museum in Hamar. Explore historic locomotives, hear fascinating stories about railways and transportation, and even hop aboard a miniature train for a delightful ride.

Address: Strandvegen 161, 2316 Hamar, Norway.

Did You Know? Innlandet boasts Galdhøpiggen, Norway's highest peak, piercing the sky at 2,469 meters. This majestic mountain challenges adventurers and draws in nature lovers with its breathtaking panoramas.

Shopping Guide:

Husfliden Stores: Immerse yourself in Norwegian handicrafts at Husfliden stores scattered throughout the region. Find hand-knitted sweaters, traditional wood carvings, and woven textiles, all made with skill and a deep appreciation for local heritage.

Jatta Gårdsbryggeri: For beer enthusiasts, Gjøvik Gårdsbryggeri offers a delightful shopping experience. Explore their craft beers, brewed with local ingredients and passion, and even take a brewery tour to learn about the brewing process.

Address: Rogstadmyra 19, 4020 Stavanger, Norway.

Sports and Leisure:

Hiking and Cycling: Innlandet is a paradise for outdoor enthusiasts, with its countless hiking trails through pristine landscapes and scenic cycling routes for all levels. Conquer challenging mountain paths in Jotunheimen, explore rolling hills in Rondane, or enjoy leisurely cycling alongside Lake Mjøsa.

Fishing and Kayaking: Cast your line in crystal-clear lakes and rivers or glide across the tranquil waters of Lake Mjøsa by kayak. Innlandet's abundance of waterways gives fishing enthusiasts and paddlers endless opportunities.

Whitewater Rafting and Skiing: Seek adrenaline thrills on the rapids of Gudbrandsdalslågen River or conquer the slopes of Hafjell and Skeikampen ski resorts. Innlandet provides adventure for all tastes, from mild whitewater rafting experiences to challenging downhill ski runs.

Golfing and Wildlife Watching: Enjoy a game of golf amidst breathtaking scenery at courses like Hafjell Golf and Trysil Golf or embark on a wildlife-watching adventure in search of moose, reindeer, and other fascinating creatures.

Horseback Riding and Snowshoeing: Explore the region on horseback, following scenic trails through valleys and forests, or experience the magic of winter landscapes on a snowshoeing adventure. Innlandet offers unique ways to connect with nature and create lasting memories.

Accommodations:

From cozy cabins nestled in the mountains to guesthouses in idyllic villages and modern hotels in major towns, Innlandet offers a diverse range of accommodations to suit every budget and travel style.

Lillehammer: Indulge in luxury with panoramic views at Scandic Victoria Hotel, a modern haven perched on the shores of Lake Mjøsa. For budget-conscious travelers, Lillehammer Vandrerhjem offers comfortable hostel accommodations and a friendly atmosphere.

Scandic Victoria Lillehammer Address: Nymosvingen 3, 2609 Lillehammer, Norway.

Lillehammer Vandrerhjem Address: Jernbanestasjon, Jernbanetorget 2, 2609 Lillehammer, Norway.

Jotunheimen National Park: The rustic charm and breathtaking mountain vistas at Gjendesheim Turisthytte, a traditional mountain lodge offering comfortable dorm beds and delicious meals, promise a down-to-earth, affordable experience. For a more luxurious experience, Spiterstulen Turisthytte boasts stunning scenery and gourmet dining options. Camping enthusiasts can pitch their tents at Memurubu campsite, surrounded by the majesty of Jotunheimen peaks.

Gjendesheim Turisthytte Address: Gjendevegen 200, 2683 Tessanden, Norway.

Spiterstulen Turisthytte Address: Visdalsveien 1710, 2688 Lom, Norway.

Memurubu Address: 2686 Lom, Norway.

Rondane National Park: Find tranquility and cozy comfort at Rondane Høyfjellshotell, a family-run lodge with panoramic views and traditional Norwegian meals. For a unique experience, try Rondane Gjestegard, a working farm offering guest rooms and authentic rural experiences.

Rondane Høyfjellshotell Address: Rondanevegen 1264, 2674 Otta, Norway.

Rondane Gjestegard Address: Rondeveien 34, 3477 Sollia, Norway.

Lake Mjøsa: Unwind at Quality Hotel Strand Gjøvik, near the lake with comfortable spacious rooms with all the facilities you may need. For a budget-friendly option, stay at Gjøvik Hotel Hovdetun, which offers private rooms and gender-segregated dorms with exceptional amenities.

Quality Hotel Strand Gjøvik Address: Elvegata 3-4, 2815 Gjøvik, Norway.

Gjøvik Hotel Hovdetun Address: Parkvegen 8, 2819 Gjøvik, Norway.

Innlandet's charm extends beyond hotels and hostels. Consider specialized Airbnb stays in traditional farmhouses, cabins dotting the lake shores, or even yurts offering the ultimate off-the-grid experience. Choose the accommodation that resonates with your travel style and budget to create your perfect Innlandet adventure.

Eastern Norway has woven a spell on your senses, leaving you with memories packaged in laughter, adrenaline, and the quiet peace of nature's embrace. From scaling snow-capped peaks to strolling through fairytale-like villages, you've embraced the essence of this diverse region. Now, carry this Nordic magic with you, a reminder of the endless possibilities that lie within the heart of Scandinavia. New adventures await, hidden paths beckon, and stories yet untold whisper from the windswept mountains and shimmering fjords.

Chapter 5: Southern Norway (Sørlandet)

Open your map, cast your gaze south, and let your spirit drift to where the Skagerrak welcomes you to Southern Norway, a land where sun-kissed beaches melt into emerald valleys. Prepare to find towns pulse with vibrant culture, and the echoes of Viking sagas mingle with the cries of gulls riding the salty breeze. Once known as the separate kingdoms of Vest-Agder and Aust-Agder, this region united in 2020 under the banner of Agder, weaving itself into a captivating whole.

Sørlandet.[26]

Southern Norway is a medley of sea and sky, where turquoise waters lap against rugged coastlines, and lush forests drape rolling hills like a verdant cloak. But beyond the natural splendor, Southern Norway's warm embrace welcomes you to its picturesque towns. In this chapter, you'll discover the heart of Southern Norway, explore its hidden gems, uncover its rich culture and history, and savor the flavors that make this region a haven for travelers seeking both serenity and exhilaration.

Vest Agder: Sunshine, Seafood, and Soulful Shores

Nestled where the Skagerrak meets the Norwegian coastline, Vest Agder unveils a kaleidoscope of sun-kissed beaches, quaint towns, and vibrant coastal life. From the bustling energy of Kristiansand to the tranquil whisper of the Sørlandet archipelago, this southern gem beckons you to trade your worries for seashells and embrace the rhythm of the ocean breeze.

Historical Background:

Viking sagas echo across the rolling hills of Vest Agder, whispering tales of ancient settlements and intrepid seafarers. Kristiansand, founded in the 17th century as a fortress town, flourished into a bustling trade center, leaving behind a legacy of wooden houses and vibrant culture. Fishing villages scattered along the coast tell stories of generations who lived in harmony with the sea, their traditions woven into the fabric of the region. Today, Vest Agder celebrates its rich heritage, offering a glimpse into the past while embracing the spirit of modern Scandinavia.

Did You Know? Vest Agder houses Lindesnes Lighthouse, the oldest operational lighthouse in Norway, standing sentinel since 1655. Its powerful beam has guided countless souls through treacherous waters, earning it the moniker "Norway's southernmost eye."

Main Attractions:

Kristiansand: Dive into the city's vibrant energy, exploring Posebyen (Old Town) with its colorful houses and intriguing shops. Wander along Bystranda, a pristine beach perfect for sunbathing and watersports. Immerse yourself in the playful chaos of Kristiansand Dyrepark (Zoo and Amusement Park), where thrilling rides and adorable animals promise family fun. Don't miss the mesmerizing light show projected onto the majestic Kristiansand Cathedral for a truly awe-inspiring experience.

As of the writing of this book, you can visit Kristiansand at any time during your trip. The Kristiansand Dyrepark is open on Monday to Friday from 10 am to 4 pm and Saturday and Sunday from 10 am to 6 pm. The

Kristiansand Cathedral is open from Monay to Friday from 10 am to 5 pm and is closed on Saturday and Sunday. However, please always double-check the opening hours online should there have been any slight change in their schedule.

Kristiansand Dyrepark Address: Kardemomme By, 4609 Kristiansand, Norway.

Kristiansand Cathedral Address: Gyldenloves gate 9. 4611 Kristiansand, Norway.

Immerse yourself in the playful chaos of Kristiansand Dyrepark.[27]

Lindesnes Lighthouse: Climb the 109 steps to the top of Lindesnes Lighthouse and be rewarded with breathtaking panoramas of the North Sea. Learn about the lighthouse's fascinating history and feel the pulse of the ocean as it crashes against the rugged coastline.

As of the writing of this book, the normal opening hours are daily from 10 am till 5 pm, but please always double-check the opening hours online should there have been any slight change in their schedule.

Address: Lindesnesveien 1139, 4521 Lindesnes, Norway.

Climb the 166 steps to the top of Lindesnes Lighthouse and be rewarded with breathtaking panoramas of the North Sea.[28]

Mandal: Sail into the "City of Sails," where wooden houses line the banks of the Mandalselva River and picturesque beaches beckon for strolls. Explore the bustling harbor, sample fresh seafood at the Fiskelaget Mandal (Mandal Fish Market), and delve into the town's maritime heritage at the Mandal Museum.

As of the writing of this book, the normal opening hours daily are all 24 hours of the day. The opening hours for Fiskelaget Mandal are Monday to Friday from 6 am to 5 pm, Saturday from 7 am to 4 pm, and closed on Sunday. The opening hours for the Mandal Musum is every day from 11 am to 5 pm. However, please always double-check the opening hours online should there have been any slight change in their schedule.

Fiskelaget Address: Sommerkroveien 5, 4515 Mandal, Norway.

Mandal Museum Address: Store Elvegate 5, 4514 Mandal, Norway.

Sail into the "City of Sails," where wooden houses line the banks of the Mandalselva River and picturesque beaches beckon for strolls.[29]

Sørlandet Archipelago: Embark on island-hopping adventures in this idyllic archipelago, dotted with pristine beaches, rocky islets, and fishing villages. Kayak through hidden coves, rent a sailboat for a breezy adventure, or cast your line and savor the bounty of the sea.

As of the writing of this book, the normal opening hours daily are all 24 hours of the day, but please always double-check the opening hours online should there have been any slight change in their schedule.

Transport:

Vest Agder is easily accessible by train, bus, and plane. Kristiansand Airport serves as the region's main hub, connecting it to domestic and international destinations. Public transportation within major towns is efficient and affordable. Intercity travel is well-connected by trains and buses, and a network of scenic roads crisscrosses the region, offering opportunities for road trips. Frequent ferry services operate between mainland towns and several islands, creating a seamless archipelago experience.

Experiences:

Viking Ship Cruise: Sail the Skagerrak aboard a replica Viking ship, feeling the wind in your hair and immersing yourself in the world of these legendary seafarers. Learn about Viking navigation, try your hand at rowing, and experience the thrill of conquering the waves like those fearless explorers of long ago.

Mandal Canal Boat Tour: Glide along the tranquil Mandalselva River, soaking in the scenic beauty of the surrounding countryside. Observe diverse birdlife, learn about the canal's history, and savor the serenity of this peaceful waterway.

Culinary Tour of Kristiansand: Embark on a delicious journey through Kristiansand's food scene, sampling delicacies from bustling marketplaces to Michelin-starred restaurants. Discover fresh seafood caught just off the coast, indulge in traditional Norwegian fare, and savor the region's unique culinary identity.

Lindesnes Lighthouse Sunset Climb: Witness a breathtaking spectacle as the sun dips below the horizon, painting the sky in fiery hues from the vantage point of Lindesnes Lighthouse. Feel the cool ocean breeze on your face, listen to the waves whispering secrets, and let the magic of the moment wash over you.

Sørlandet Archipelago Kayaking Adventure: Explore hidden coves and untouched shores by kayak, weaving through the labyrinth of the Sørlandet archipelago. Enjoy the quiet solitude of the sea, listen to the gentle lapping of water against the rocks, and experience the serenity of nature at its finest.

Did You Know? Kristiansand boasts Scandinavia's largest reptile house, home to fascinating creatures like Komodo dragons and boa constrictors. Prepare to be amazed by the slithering beauty and intriguing world of reptiles.

Family Fun:

Kristiansand Dyrepark: Let your inner child loose at Kristiansand Dyrepark, where rollercoasters, adorable animal encounters, and captivating shows promise endless entertainment. Scream your lungs out on the Kardemomme By train, get lost in the magical world of Hakkebakkeskogen, and marvel at the majestic tigers and playful monkeys. Dyrepark offers a day of laughter, wonder, and memories that will last a lifetime.

Address: Kardemomme By, 4609 Kristiansand, Norway.

Tropicana Badeland: Make a splash at Tropicana Badeland, which features thrilling slides, lazy rivers, and wave pools for all ages. Slide down the heart-stopping Black Hole, relax in the jacuzzi under the palm trees, and let loose in the playful atmosphere of this aquatic paradise.

Address: Dalevegen 1, 3550 Gol, Norway.

Mandal Museum: Embark on a family-friendly journey through time at the Mandal Museum, where interactive exhibits and playful displays bring history to life. Learn about the region's maritime heritage, discover the secrets of the Vikings, and let your children explore the world through hands-on activities.

Address: Store Elvegate 5, 4514 Mandal, Norway.

Where to Eat:

Fisketorget (Kristiansand Fish Market): Savor the freshest seafood in a vibrant atmosphere at Fisketorget. Sample succulent oysters, indulge in steaming fish soup, and try local delicacies like Skrei (Norwegian cod) prepared following traditional recipes.

Address: Gravane 6, 4610 Kristiansand, Norway.

Restaurant Under (Lindesnes): Escape the land and enjoy a a delicious meal at Restaurant Under, located 5.5 meters below sea level. Savor delicious dishes made with high-quality ingredients while enjoying a view of the ocean.

Address: 4521 Baly, Norway.

Shopping Guide:

Posebyen (Kristiansand Old Town): Wander through the streets of Posebyen, lined with colorful houses and independent shops. Discover unique crafts, locally designed clothing, and beautiful souvenirs to take home a piece of Vest Agder's charm.

Mandal Market: Browse the stalls of the vibrant Mandal Market, overflowing with fresh produce, local crafts, and handmade treasures. Find the perfect souvenir, sample delicious local treats, and experience the authentic pulse of the town.

Address: Store Elvegate 31, 4514 Mandal, Norway.

Husfliden Stores: Immerse yourself in Norwegian craftsmanship at Husfliden stores scattered throughout the region. Find hand-knitted sweaters, traditional wood carvings, and woven textiles, all handcrafted in traditional motifs.

Kristiansand Sandens: Explore the largest shopping center in Southern Norway, Kristiansand Sandens, offering a diverse range of stores from international brands to local boutiques. Find everything you need, from clothing and accessories to electronics and groceries, under one roof.

Address: Tollbodgata 14, 4611 Kristiansand, Norway.

Entertainment:

Kristiansand Symphony Orchestra: Immerse yourself in the world of music at a concert by the Kristiansand Symphony Orchestra, renowned for its captivating performances and diverse repertoire. Experience the magic of classical music in the elegant setting of the Kilden Performing Arts Centre.

Address: Sjolystveien 2, 4610 Kristiansand, Norway.

Grimstad Byfestival (Grimstad City Festival): Immerse yourself in the festive spirit of the Grimstad Byfestival, held annually in July. Experience live music, street performances, art installations, and a vibrant street food market, all set against the picturesque backdrop of Grimstad Harbor.

Mandal Jazzfestival: Let the rhythm of jazz wash over you at the renowned Mandal Jazzfestival, held every year in August. Hear world-class musicians from across the globe perform in various venues, creating a truly unforgettable musical experience.

Nightlife in Kristiansand: Dance the night away at one of Kristiansand's lively nightclubs or enjoy a relaxed evening with live music at a cozy bar. Explore the vibrant streets of Posebyen with its trendy bars and pubs, or head to the harborside for a unique atmosphere.

Sports and Leisure:

Hiking and Cycling: Lace up your boots or hop on your bike and explore the scenic trails that crisscross Vest Agder. Hike through lush forests, conquer challenging mountain paths, or cycle along the bracing coastline, enjoying breathtaking views and fresh air.

Kayaking and Sailing: Embrace the spirit of the sea by kayaking through the tranquil waters of the Sørlandet archipelago or renting a sailboat to explore hidden coves and secluded beaches. Feel the wind in your hair and the sun on your skin, creating lasting memories on the open water.

Golfing: Swing your clubs at one of Vest Agder's picturesque golf courses, offering stunning views and challenging layouts. Choose from championship-level courses like Sørlandet Golf Club or local greens, perfect for golfers of all skill levels.

Fishing: Cast your line in the rich fishing grounds of Vest Agder, teeming with cod, salmon, and other sea bounty. Whether you're a seasoned angler or a curious beginner, fishing trips and charters are the perfect opportunity to connect with nature and enjoy the thrill of the catch.

Surfing and Stand-Up Paddleboarding: Ride the waves at Agder's pristine beaches, known for their consistent swells and vibrant surfing community. Rent a board, learn from experienced instructors, or simply unwind on a paddleboard, soaking in the beauty of the coastline.

Accommodations:

Vest Agder offers diverse accommodations to suit every budget and travel style. From luxurious seaside resorts and guesthouses in historic towns to cozy cabins nestled amidst picturesque landscapes and campsites offering an immersive nature experience, you'll find the perfect place to rest your head after a day of exploring.

Kristiansand: Indulge in luxury at Hotel Caledonien, offering panoramic city views and world-class amenities. For a more intimate experience, check into one of Posebyen's boutique hotels housed in historical buildings. Budget travelers can find comfortable and convenient options at hostels and guest houses.

Hotel Caledonien Address: Vestre Strandgate 7, 4610 Kristiansand, Norway.

Lindesnes: Experience the rugged beauty of the southernmost tip of Norway at Lindesnes Gjestehus, a family-run guest house that boasts stunning ocean views. Alternatively, the Lindesnes Lighthouse offers overnight stays within its tower, perfect for adventurers seeking an unusual experience.

Lindesnes Gjestehus Address: Hollen, 4521 Spangereid, Norway.

Mandal: Choose one of the town's traditional wooden houses converted into guesthouses for a cozy atmosphere. Budget travelers can find comfortable options at camping grounds and hostels.

Sørlandet Archipelago: Immerse yourself in island life at one of the archipelago's idyllic beaches. Rent a cabin with private beachfront access, or book a stay at a small, family-run guesthouse tucked away on a secluded island. For a truly exceptional experience, consider renting a houseboat and exploring the islands at your own pace.

Vest Agder beckons you with its sun-kissed shores, vibrant culture, and endless opportunities for adventure. Whether you're seeking family fun, historical insights, or a dose of coastal serenity, this southern gem promises experiences that will stay with you long after you've packed your bags.

Aust Agder: Where Coastal Charm Meets Rich Heritage

Aust Agder is nestled between the sparkling Skagerrak and rolling green hills. From the bustling streets of Arendal to the serene coves of hidden islands, this southern Norwegian gem invites you to trade city lights for the warmth of bonfires and the salty kiss of the sea.

Historical Background:

Vikings carved their legacy onto the rugged coastline of Aust Agder, leaving behind burial mounds and runestones that echo with whispers of their voyages and battles. Fishing villages sprang up along the shores, their traditions embedded into the fabric of life in towns like Grimstad and Lillesand. In the 17th century, Arendal blossomed into a maritime powerhouse, its shipyards and bustling harbor marking a new chapter in the region's story. Today, Aust Agder celebrates its rich heritage, embracing ancient stories while thriving as a modern haven for those seeking authenticity and coastal charm.

Main Attractions:

Arendal: Join the lively spirit of Arendal, exploring its well-preserved Old Town with colorful wooden houses and cobbled streets. Climb the steps of the iconic Arendal Town Hall for panoramic views and find solace in the peaceful Trinity Church. From Arendal, explore the surrounding beauty of the Nidelva River, or lose yourself in the tranquil wilderness of Raet National Park.

As of the writing of this book, the normal opening hours are every day all 24 hours of the day. The opening hours for the Arendal Town Hall is Monday to Friday from 9 am to 3 pm, closed on Saturday and Sunday. The opening hours for the Trinity Church are Tuesday to Saturday from 11:30 am to 3:30 pm. However, please always double-check the opening hours online should there have been any slight change in their schedule.

Arendal Town Hall Address: Sam Eydes plass 2, 4836 Arendal, Norway.

Trinity Church Address: Kirkebakken 1, 4836 Arendal, Norway.

Raet National Park Address: Hove, Arendal, Norway.

Join the lively spirit of Arendal, exploring its well-preserved Old Town with colorful wooden houses and cobbled streets.[30]

Grimstad: Soak in the charm of Grimstad, a town where maritime traditions mingle with cultural vibrancy. Visit the Maritime Museum and embark on a journey through the region's seafaring past. Marvel at the intricate architecture of Grimstad Church, and lose yourself in the historic harbor. Delve into the town's literary legacy at the Ibsenhuset, dedicated to the renowned playwright Henrik Ibsen.

The opening hours for the Maritime Museum are every day from 11 am to 4 pm. The opening hours for Ibsenhuset are every day from 11 am to 4 pm. However, please always double-check the opening hours online should there have been any slight change in their schedule.

Maritime Museum Address: Hasselldalen 3, Grimstad, Norway.

Grimstad Church Address: Kirkegaten 16, 4878 Grimstad, Norway.

Ibsenhuset Address: Henrik Ibsens gate 14, 4878 Grimstad, Norway.

Soak in the charm of Grimstad, a town where maritime traditions mingle with cultural vibrancy.[31]

Island Hopping: Embark on an island-hopping adventure through the captivating archipelago. Kayak between secluded coves on Tromøya, known for its idyllic beaches and hidden coves. Discover the historical treasures of Hisøya, where ancient burial mounds stand watch over the coastline. Explore the vibrant fishing village of Justøya, savor fresh seafood on Sandøya, or simply find your hidden paradise on one of the countless islets.

Discover the historical treasures of Hisøya, where ancient burial mounds stand watch over the coastline.[32]

Coastal Gems: Lillesand beckons with its sandy beaches, harbor, and lively summer festivals. Hike the coastal paths of Tvedestrand, where rugged cliffs meet gentle bays, or wander through the historic streets of Risør, known for its well-preserved wooden houses and hidden hiking trails. These coastal towns offer a serene escape, perfect for those seeking a taste of traditional Norwegian life and breathtaking natural beauty.

Hike the coastal paths of Tvedestrand, where rugged cliffs meet gentle bays, or wander through the historic streets of Risør, known for its well-preserved wooden houses and hidden hiking trails.[33]

Transport:

Aust Agder is easily accessible by train, bus, and plane. Kristiansand Airport, the region's main hub, connects it to domestic and international destinations. Public transportation within major towns is efficient and affordable. Intercity travel is well-connected by trains and buses, and scenic roads crisscross the region, offering opportunities for road trips. Ferry services operate regularly between mainland towns and islands, making island hopping a breeze.

Did You Know? Aust Agder boasts Norway's largest archipelago, with over 500 islands dotting the coastline. These hidden gems offer secluded beaches, untouched nature, and a window into a timeless way of life.

Experiences:

Viking Ship Cruise: Sail the Skagerrak aboard a replica Viking ship, feeling the wind in your hair and immersing yourself in the world of these legendary seafarers. Learn about Viking navigation, try your hand at rowing, and experience the thrill of conquering the waves like these fearless explorers.

Grimstad Byfestival: Immerse yourself in the festive spirit of the Grimstad Byfestival, held annually in July. Experience live music, street performances, art installations, and a vibrant street food market, all set against the picturesque backdrop of Grimstad Harbor.

Arendal Canal Boat Tour: Glide along the tranquil Nidelva River, soaking in the scenic beauty of the surrounding countryside. Observe diverse birdlife, learn about the history of the canal, and savor the serenity of this peaceful waterway.

Raet National Park Wildlife Safari: Embark on a guided safari through the unique landscape of Raet National Park, home to diverse birdlife, seals, and even wild deer. Learn about the park's delicate ecosystem and witness the beauty of nature untouched.

Island Hopping Food Tour: Discover the culinary delights of the archipelago on a delicious island-hopping food tour. Savor fresh seafood caught just off the coast, indulge in traditional Norwegian dishes like pølser (sausages) and brunost (brown cheese) made with local ingredients, and sample homemade pastries while enjoying the breathtaking scenery.

Family Fun:

Dyreparken Kristiansand: Take a day trip to Dyreparken Kristiansand, a popular zoo and amusement park located just outside of Kristiansand.

Let your inner child loose on thrilling rollercoasters, meet adorable animals, and enjoy captivating shows, creating lasting memories for the whole family.

Grimstad Maritime Museum: Embark on a family-friendly journey through time at the Grimstad Maritime Museum, where interactive exhibits and playful displays bring history to life. Learn about the town's shipbuilding past, climb aboard a replica Viking ship, and discover the secrets of the sea.

Lillesand Beach Day: Build sandcastles, splash in the waves, and soak up the sun on the pristine shores of Lillesand Beach. This family-friendly beach offers gentle waves, lifeguards on duty, and plenty of space for picnics and games, making it the perfect spot for creating lasting memories with your family.

Did You Know? Norway's first Christmas tree was lit in Grimstad in 1848, sparking a tradition that now warms hearts across the globe.

Where to Eat:

Blom Restaurant (Arendal): Enjoy a delicious meal at Blom Restaurant. The dishes at this restaurant are a blend between modern trends and traditional Norwegian meals. Dine at this restaurant for a beautiful experience in a welcoming place.

Address: Langbryggen 9, 4841 Arendal, Norway.

Symbio Bistro (Grimstad): If you're looking for a casual dining experience, Symbio Bistro is the right place to go. Choose your favorite dish from a diverse menu serving pasta, sandwiches, and fresh salads while enjoying the wonderful service.

Shopping Guide:

Alti Arendal (Arendal): In the heart of Arendal lies Alti Arendal, a shopping center with a wide variety of shops with everything you may need. There are also several cafes and restaurants for you to experience.

Address: Vesterveien 4, 4836 Arendal, Norway.

Oddensenteret (Grimstad): Wander through Oddensenteret, a small, charming shopping center along the water. This shopping center has a great selection of stores and stalls selling locally produced fruit, vegetables, and bakery items all year round.

Address: Odden 1D, 4876 Grimstad, Norway.

Tvedestrand Bygdesentrum (Tvedestrand Town Center): Explore the bustling market square of Tvedestrand Bygdesentrum, offering fresh produce, local crafts, and delicious treats. Sample traditional Norwegian cheeses, stock up on homemade jams and honey, and find the perfect souvenir to take home.

Address: Tvedestrand, Norway.

Lillesand Senter (Lillesand): Find everything you need under one roof at Lillesand Senter, which offers a wide range of stores from international brands to local boutiques. Browse for clothing, accessories, homeware, and electronics, all while enjoying the convenience of a modern shopping center.

Address: Senterveien 30, 4790 Lillesand, Norway.

Entertainment:

Kilden Performing Arts Centre (Kristiansand): Immerse yourself in the world of music, theatre, and dance at the Kilden Performing Arts Centre, a vibrant hub for cultural events. Witness world-class orchestras, captivating dance performances, and thought-provoking theatre productions, all within a stunning architectural masterpiece.

Address: Sjolystveien 2, 4610 Kristiansand, Norway.

Grimstad Bykino (Grimstad Cinema): Catch the latest blockbusters or discover independent gems at Grimstad Bykino, a cinema housed in a historic building. Enjoy a cozy movie night with popcorn and refreshments, or attend special screenings and film festivals throughout the year.

Address: Storgaten 33, 4876 Grimstad, Norway.

Arendal Live (Arendal Concert Hall): Experience the magic of live music at Arendal Live, a renowned concert hall hosting diverse performances from local bands to international stars. From jazz and classical to rock and pop, there's something for everyone to enjoy in this intimate and acoustically stunning venue.

Address: Sam Eydes Plass 2, 4836 Arendal, Norway.

Risør Kammermusikkfestival (Risør Chamber Music Festival): Drown in the world of classical music during the prestigious Risør Kammermusikkfestival held annually in July. Listen to renowned musicians perform in intimate settings like historic churches and concert halls, creating an unforgettable musical experience.

Sports and Leisure:

Hiking and Cycling: Lace up your boots or hop on your bike and explore the scenic trails that crisscross Aust Agder. Hike through lush forests along the coast, conquer challenging mountain paths in Raet National Park, or cycle along the picturesque Nidelva River, enjoying breathtaking views and fresh air.

Kayaking and Stand-Up Paddleboarding: Embrace the spirit of the sea by kayaking through the calm waters of the archipelago or exploring hidden coves on a stand-up paddleboard. Rent a board, join a guided tour, or simply enjoy the serenity of gliding across the water surrounded by stunning scenery.

Fishing: Cast your line in the rich fishing grounds of Aust Agder, known for its abundance of cod, salmon, and other bounty from the sea. Whether you're a seasoned angler or a curious beginner, fishing trips and charters offer the perfect opportunity to connect with nature and enjoy the thrill of the catch.

Golfing: Swing your clubs at one of Aust Agder's picturesque golf courses, offering stunning views and challenging layouts. Choose from championship-level courses like Arendal Golf Club or the unique island course of Fevik Golfklubb, perfect for golfers of all skill levels.

Birdwatching: Aust Agder is a haven for birdwatchers, with its diverse birdlife ranging from majestic eagles and playful seabirds to colorful songbirds and migratory species. Explore the Raet National Park wetlands, visit the birdwatching towers along the coast, or simply keep your eyes peeled for feathered friends while exploring the region.

Accommodations:

Aust Agder offers a range of accommodations for every budget and travel style. From luxurious waterfront hotels and guesthouses in historical towns to cozy cabins nestled amidst picturesque landscapes and campsites offering an immersive nature experience, you'll find the perfect place to rest your head after a day of exploring.

Arendal: Indulge in luxury at the Clarion Hotel, offering panoramic city views and world-class amenities. For a more intimate experience, choose one of Arendal's boutique hotels housed in historic buildings in the Old Town. Budget travelers will find comfortable options at hostels and guest houses.

Clarion Hotel Tyholmen Address: Teaterplassen 2, 4801 Tylholmen, Arendal, Norway.

Grimstad: Embrace the charm of a maritime town at the Topcamp Bie, a campsite in Grimstad with spacious cabins and multiple amenities including free Wi-Fi, a pool, and a restaurant. Topcamp Bie is in a central location, keeping you near any attractions you may want to see.

Tompcamp Bie Address: Arendalsveien 85, 4878 Grimstad, Norway.

Islands: Experience island life at one of the many guesthouses or holiday homes scattered across the archipelago. Find your private cabin on a secluded island, rent a cozy cottage with a beachfront view, or opt for a stay in a traditional fishing village.

Coastal Towns: Lillesand, Tvedestrand, and Risør offer a variety of accommodation options, from comfortable hotels and family-friendly apartments to guesthouses and bed-and-breakfasts. Choose a location close to the beach or harbor for a truly immersive experience.

Aust Agder beckons you with its sun-kissed shores, vibrant culture, and endless opportunities for adventure. Whether you're seeking family fun, historical insights, or a taste of traditional Norwegian life, this southern gem promises experiences that will stay with you long after you've packed your bags.

As the sun dips below the horizon, painting the sky in fiery hues, it's time to bid farewell to Southern Norway, but not without carrying its magic in your heart. You've hiked through verdant valleys, kayaked in crystal-clear waters, and feasted on the bounty of the sea. You've wandered through towns, soaking in their vibrant culture and rich history, and you've danced to the rhythm of the waves, feeling the pulse of this unique region.

Chapter 6: Western Norway (Vestlandet)

Brace yourself for the symphony of the sea and the grandeur of glacial peaks. Welcome to Western Norway (Vestlandet), a land where valleys unfold into shimmering fjords, waterfalls cascade like liquid crystal, and the rhythm of the waves echoes tales of ancient explorers. From the bustling streets of Bergen to the silent serenity of untouched fjords, Western Norway invites you to embark on a journey where every turn promises awe-inspiring beauty.

Vestlandet.[34]

Rogaland: Where Fjord Majesty Meets Cultural Gems

Rogaland, nestled between the sparkling Skagerrak and the wild North Sea, beckons you to a symphony of contrasts. From the majestic cliffs of Lysefjordento the cobbled streets of Stavanger, this western Norwegian county promises breathtaking landscapes, captivating history, and modern vibrancy. Whether you're an adventure seeker scaling Kjeragbolten, a history buff delving into Viking sagas, or a family seeking sun and sand, Rogaland is a hidden gem waiting to be discovered.

Historical Background:

Viking legacy is found everywhere along the rugged coastline of Rogaland. Fishing villages sprouted along the fjords; their traditions are seen in towns like Stavanger and Haugesund. In the 12th century, Stavanger blossomed into a thriving trade center, its harbor buzzing with ships and its streets echoing with the clang of merchants. Today, Rogaland celebrates its rich heritage, embracing ancient stories while thriving as a modern hub for cultural diversity and outdoor adventures.

Main Attractions:

Lysefjorden: Embark on a breathtaking journey through Lysefjorden, which was carved by ancient glaciers. Marvel at the towering cliffs, including the iconic Preikestolen (Pulpit Rock), a 604-meter-tall natural pulpit offering panoramic views that will leave you breathless. Hike to the top for an unforgettable experience, or take a boat tour to witness the fjord's grandeur from below.

As of the writing of this book, the normal opening hours daily are all 24 hours of the day, but please always double-check the opening hours online should there have been any slight change in their schedule.

Embark on a breathtaking journey through Lysefjorden, a UNESCO World Heritage Site carved by ancient glaciers.[35]

Kjeragbolten: Test your nerves and defy gravity at Kjeragbolten, a boulder precariously balanced between two mountain peaks. This natural wonder, nicknamed the "pea in the pod," promises an adrenaline-pumping adventure for those seeking a challenge with a difference.

As of the writing of this book, the hike to Kjeragbolten should only be done between June 1st and September 30th of every year as it can get dangerous during the winter, but please always double-check the opening hours online should there have been any slight change in their schedule.

Address: Kjerag, 4127 Lysebotn, Norway.

Test your nerves and defy gravity at Kjeragbolten, a boulder precariously balanced between two mountain peaks.[36]

Stavanger: Dive into the streets of Stavanger, Norway's "City of Gladioli." Wander through the colorful Gamle Stavanger (Old Town), a maze of wooden houses and cobbled streets, and delve into the city's maritime history at the Stavanger Maritime Museum. Don't miss the Stavanger Cathedral, a magnificent example of Gothic architecture, and explore the vibrant art scene at the Stavanger Konserthus and Kunstmuseum.

As of the writing of this book, you can visit Stavanger and Gamle Stavanger at any time during your trip. The opening hours for the Stavanger Maritime Museum are every day from 10 am to 4 pm. The opening hours for the Stavanger Cathedral are Monday to Sunday from 11 am to 7 pm. The opening hours for the Stavanger Konserthus are Thursday from 3 pm to 6 pm and Saturday from 11 am to 3 pm. Lastly, The Stavanger Kunstmuseum is open Monday to Wednesday and Friday and Saturday from 11 am to 4 pm, Thursday from 11 am to 7 pm, and Sunday from 11 am to 5 pm.

Gamle Stavanger Address: Ovre Strandgate, 4005 Stavanger, Norway.

Stavanger Maritime Museum Address: Strandkeien 22, 4005 Stavanger, Norway.

Stavanger Cathedral Address: Haakon Vlls gate 2, 4005 Stavanger, Norway.

Stavanger Konserthus Address: Sandviga 1, 4007 Stavanger, Norway.

Stavanger Kunstmuseum Address: Henrik Ibsens gate 55, 4021 Stavanger, Norway.

Wander through the colorful Gamle Stavanger (Old Town), which is a maze of wooden houses and cobbled streets.[37]

Swords in Rock: Witness the enigmatic Swords in Rock monument, where four giant swords rise from the ground near Stavanger. The origin and meaning of this mysterious installation remain shrouded in legend, fueling your imagination as you ponder their secrets.

As of the writing of this book, the normal opening hours daily are all 24 hours of the day, but please always double-check the opening hours online should there have been any slight change in their schedule.

Address: Mollebukta, 4044 Hafrsfjord, Norway.

Witness the enigmatic Swords in Rock monument, where four giant swords rise from the ground near Stavanger.[38]

Sola Beach: Soak up the sun on the pristine shores of Sola Beach, a paradise for sunbathers, surfers, and beachcombers. Enjoy the gentle waves, build sandcastles with your family, or take a refreshing dip in the North Sea.

As of the writing of this book, the normal opening hours daily are all 24 hours of the day, but please always double-check the opening hours online should there have been any slight change in their schedule.

Address: Sola, Norway.

Soak up the sun on the pristine shores of Sola Beach, a paradise for sunbathers, surfers, and beachcombers.[39]

Transport:

Rogaland is easily accessible by plane, train, and ferry. Stavanger Airport serves as the region's main hub, connecting it to domestic and international destinations. Public transportation within Stavanger and other major towns is efficient and affordable. Intercity travel is well-connected by trains and buses, and a network of scenic roads crisscrosses the region, offering opportunities for road trips. Regular ferry services operate between mainland towns and islands, making exploration convenient and hassle-free.

Experiences:

Stavanger Food Walk: Embark on a delicious journey through Stavanger's culinary scene, sampling fresh seafood from the docks, savoring traditional Norwegian dishes like "fiskekaker" (fish cakes) and "brunost" (brown cheese), and indulging in sweet treats like "skillingsboller" (cinnamon buns).

Lysefjord Kayak Tour: Paddle through the tranquil waters of Lysefjord, enjoying the majestic silence and breathtaking scenery from a unique perspective. Witness waterfalls cascading down the cliffs, spot playful seals basking on the rocks and create lasting memories of this fjord odyssey.

Kjeragbolten Hike: Embark on a challenging but rewarding hike to Kjeragbolten, scaling rugged mountains and testing your endurance. Feel the thrill of conquering the peaks and revel in the breathtaking views that await you at the top,

Haugesund Viking Festival: Immerse yourself in the spirit of Viking history during the annual Haugesund Viking Festival. Watch warriors clad in armor recreating traditional battles and experience the sights and sounds of medieval life. Learn about Viking crafts, sample hearty Viking food, and join the festivities celebrating this region's rich heritage.

Preikestolen Sunrise Hike: Witness the magic of sunrise from the awe-inspiring peak of Preikestolen. Climb the trail under the cloak of darkness, reaching the summit just as the first rays of sunlight paint the sky with vibrant hues. Feel a sense of peace and wonder as the fjord awakens below you, bathed in the golden light of dawn.

Rogaland Fjord Cruise: Embark on a scenic cruise through the enchanting fjords of Rogaland, enjoying the serenity of the landscape and marveling at the towering cliffs and cascading waterfalls. Relax on deck, breathe in the fresh air, and capture stunning photos as you navigate this breathtaking natural wonder.

Family Fun:

Kongeparken: Let your inner child loose at Kongeparken, Norway's largest amusement park. Catch the thrill on rollercoasters, splash in water rides, explore pirate ships and Wild West towns, and create lasting memories for the whole family.

Address: Kongsgata 20, 4331 Algard, Norway.

Stavanger Maritime Museum: Take your children to an interactive exploration of Stavanger's maritime past at the Stavanger Maritime Museum. Climb aboard replica Viking ships, learn about shipbuilding techniques, and discover exciting stories of pirates and seafaring adventures.

Address: Strandkeien 22, 4005 Stavanger, Norway.

The Norwegian Children's Museum: Let your kids' imaginations run wild at The Norwegian Children's Museum in Stavanger. Play in themed exhibits, explore miniature houses, and participate in workshops that spark creativity and learning.

Address: Musegata 16, 4010 Stavanger, Norway.

Sola Strand Hotel & Resort: Enjoy a family-friendly getaway at Sola Strand Hotel & Resort, featuring a water park, kids' clubs, and plenty of activities to keep children entertained. Relax on the beach, build sandcastles, and splash in the pools while creating lasting memories with your loved ones.

Address: Axel Lunds veg 27, 4055 Sola, Noway.

Did You Know? Rogaland houses one of the world's largest collections of petroglyphs and ancient rock carvings dating back to 5000 BCE, offering a glimpse into the lives of its earliest inhabitants.

Where to Eat:

Renaa Restaurant (Stavanger): Indulge in a Michelin-starred culinary experience at Renaa Restaurant, showcasing innovative dishes crafted with local, seasonal ingredients. Savor artfully presented courses, enjoy the elegant ambiance, and treat yourself to an unforgettable dining experience.

Address: Nordbogata 8, 4006 Stavanger, Norway.

Fish & Cow (Stavanger): Experience the freshest seafood and juicy steaks at Fish & Meat, a popular casual restaurant. Dine al fresco on the bustling street or soak up the vibes indoors while enjoying delicious plates and friendly service.

Address: Skagen 3, 4001 Stavanger, Norway.

Slottet Sirdal (Sirdal): Enjoy panoramic mountain views and delectable Norwegian fare at Slottet Sirdal. Sample reindeer stew, savor fresh fish dishes, and indulge in homemade desserts while basking in the stunning scenery.

Address: Slotter 1 , 4443 Tjorhom, Norway.

Carlos' Bistro (Haugesund): Carlos' Bistro offers you a tasty detour from everyday life right in the heart of Haugesund. Savor Mediterranean cuisine in a warm atmosphere with a variety of salads, sandwiches, and main courses.

Address: Haraldsgata 131, 5527 Haugesund, Norway.

Shopping Guide:

Torget Market: Discover unique treasures at Torget. Find handcrafted jewelry, knitted sweaters, ceramics, and souvenirs with a Norwegian touch, all made with love and skill.

Address: Torget, 4006 Stavanger, Norway.

Amfi Madla (Stavanger): Find everything you need under one roof at Amfi Madla, which offers a diverse range of stores from international brands to local shops. Browse for clothing, electronics, groceries, and souvenirs, and enjoy the convenience of this modern shopping hub.

Address: Madlakrossen 7, 4042 Hafrsfjord, Norway.

Haugesund Sentrum: The bustling streets of Haugesund Sentrum offer a mix of chain stores and independent shops. Find everything from clothing and accessories to local crafts and souvenirs, and enjoy the vibrant atmosphere while exploring this charming town.

Address: Strandgata 171, 5521 Haugesund, Norway.

Did You Know? Stavanger was awarded the European Capital of Culture title in 2008, a testament to its vibrant art scene and commitment to preserving its rich cultural heritage.

Entertainment:

Stavanger Konserthus: Experience the magic of live music at Stavanger Konserthus, a concert hall renowned for hosting diverse performances. From classical orchestras to jazz concerts and contemporary music, there's something for everyone to enjoy in this acoustically stunning venue.

Address: Sandviga 1, 4007 Stavanger, Norway.

Rogaland Theatre: Immerse yourself in the world of theatre at Rogaland Theatre, showcasing a vibrant program of productions throughout the year. Enjoy dramas, comedies, musicals, and children's performances, all staged in a modern and innovative setting.

Address: Teaterveien 1, 4005 Stavanger, Norway.

Rogaland Kunstsenter (Stavanger): Explore visual arts at Rogaland Kunstmuseum, showcasing a diverse collection of Norwegian and international art. Wander through galleries with exhibits spanning centuries, discover the works of renowned artists, and participate in engaging exhibitions and workshops.

Address: Nytorget 17, 4013 Stavanger, Norway.

Haugesund Byfestival (Haugesund Town Festival): Immerse yourself in the festive spirit of the annual Haugesund Byfestival, held in June. Witness vibrant parades, enjoy live music on street stages, sample delicious food from local vendors, and join in the fun as the town comes alive with celebration.

Sports and Leisure:

Fishing: Cast your line in the rich fishing grounds of Rogaland, known for its abundance of cod, salmon, and other bounty from the sea. Whether you're a seasoned angler or a curious beginner, fishing trips and charters offer the perfect opportunity to connect with nature and enjoy the thrill of the catch.

Golfing: Swing your clubs at one of Rogaland's picturesque golf courses, offering stunning views and challenging layouts. Choose from championship-level courses like Stavanger Golf Club or Haugesund Golf Club, which are perfect for golfers of all skill levels.

Stavanger Golf Club Address: Longebakke 45, 4042 Hafrsfjord, Norway.

Haugesund Golf Club Address: Eikjevegen 205, 5541 Kolnes, Norway.

Surfing: Catch some waves at Sola Beach, a popular spot for surfers of all levels. Enjoy consistent swells, rent equipment, and take lessons from experienced instructors as you conquer the waves of the North Sea.

Accommodations:

Stavanger: Indulge in luxury at Radisson Blu Atlantic Hotel, which has panoramic city views and world-class amenities. For a more intimate experience, check into one of Stavanger's boutique hotels housed in historic buildings in the Old Town.

Radisson Blu Atlantic Hotel Address: Olav V s gate 3, 4005 Stavanger, Norway.

Haugesund: Embrace the vibrant atmosphere of Haugesund by staying at the centrally located Quality Hotel Maritim, overlooking the harbor. Alternatively, choose one of the town's cozy guesthouses or family-friendly apartments.

Quality Hotel Maritim Address: Asbygata 3, 5528 Haugesund, Norway.

Fjords and Mountains: Experience the peace of the fjords and the majesty of the mountains by staying in one of the many cabins or lodges scattered throughout the region. Find your private retreat with stunning views, or opt for a comfortable hotel in a picturesque village.

Sola Beach: Enjoy a beachside getaway at Sola Strand Hotel & Resort, offering family-friendly amenities and direct access to the beach. For a more laid-back experience, choose one of the nearby campsites and immerse yourself in the beauty of the coastline.

Sola Strand Hotel and Resort Address: Axel Lunds veg 27, 4055 Sola, Norway.

Rogaland promises an unforgettable tapestry of adventures, from navigating breathtaking fjords and scaling rugged mountains to delving into Viking history and savoring fresh seafood.

Vestland: Where Fjords Kiss the Sky and Culture Whispers in the Wind

Vestland, a canvas painted by windswept fjords and vibrant cityscapes, beckons you to a land where Viking sagas echo in glacial valleys and sun-drenched orchards spill onto shimmering waters. This western Norwegian region is a symphony of contrasts, where the majesty of nature dances alongside the charm of ancient towns, each step revealing a new verse in its captivating story.

Historical Background:

In the 12th century, Bergen blossomed into a powerful Hanseatic trading center, its merchants weaving a network of commerce across Europe. Today, Vestland celebrates its rich heritage, embracing ancient stories while thriving as a modern hub for cultural vibrancy and fjord escapades.

Main Attractions:

Bergen: Dive into the vibrant streets of Bergen, Norway's "City of Rain." Explore the iconic Bryggen Wharf, a UNESCO World Heritage site lined with colorful wooden houses that once housed Hanseatic merchants. Climb the Fløyen Mountain for panoramic city views, delve into Viking history at the Bergenhus Fortress, and lose yourself in the world-class art collections of the Kode Art Museums of Bergen.

As of the writing of this book, you can visit the Bryggen Wharf and Fløyen Mountain at any time during your trip. The opening hours for the Bergenhus Fortress are every day from 6 am to 11 pm. The opening hours for the Kode Art Museums of Bergen are Tuesday to Friday from 10 am to 6 pm, Saturday and Sunday from 10 am to 4 pm, and closed on Monday. However, please always double-check the opening hours online should there have been any slight change in their schedule.

Bergenhus Fortress Address: 5003 Bergen, Norway.

Lysverket Address: Rasmus Meyers alle 9. 5015 Bergen, Norway.

Dive into the vibrant streets of Bergen, Norway's "City of Rain." [40]

Hardangerfjord: Witness the natural splendor of Hardangerfjord, known as the "Kingdom of Waterfalls." Hike through fruit orchards, kayak tranquil waters, and marvel at the Folgefonna glacier, Europe's largest mainland glacier. Don't miss the Vøringsfossen waterfall, cascading 182 meters into the fjord, a spectacle that will leave you speechless.

As of the writing of this book, the normal opening hours daily are all 24 hours of the day, but please always double-check the opening hours online should there have been any slight change in their schedule.

Folgefonna National Park Address: Skalafjaero 17, 5470 Rosendal, Norway.

Voringsfossen Waterfall Address: 5785 Voringsfoss, Norway.

Witness the natural splendor of Hardangerfjord, known as the "Kingdom of Waterfalls." [41]

Sognefjord: Embark on a journey through the majesty of Sognefjord, the longest fjord in Norway. Cruise through towering cliffs and past villages, witness glaciers calving into the icy depths, and soak in the serenity of this awe-inspiring natural wonder.

As of the writing of this book, the normal opening hours daily are all 24 hours of the day, but please always double-check the opening hours online should there have been any slight change in their schedule.

Embark on a journey through the majesty of Sognefjord, a UNESCO World Heritage site and the longest fjord in Norway.[42]

Nærøyfjord: Navigate the narrow passage of Nærøyfjord, a UNESCO World Heritage site and a branch of the Sognefjord. Feel dwarfed by the towering cliffs that plunge into the water, marvel at cascading waterfalls, and witness the unique beauty of this dramatic landscape.

As of the writing of this book, the normal opening hours daily are all 24 hours of the day, but please always double-check the opening hours online should there have been any slight change in their schedule.

Navigate the narrow passage of Nærøyfjord, a UNESCO World Heritage site and a branch of the Sognefjord.[43]

Jostedalsbreen National Park: Immerse yourself in the pristine wilderness of Jostedalsbreen National Park, home to the largest glacier in mainland Europe. Hike on glaciers, explore ice caves, and witness the raw power of nature at its most awe-inspiring.

As of the writing of this book, the normal opening hours daily are all 24 hours of the day, but please always double-check the opening hours online should there have been any slight change in their schedule.

Address: 6799 Fosnes, Norway.

Immerse yourself in the pristine wilderness of Jostedalsbreen National Park, home to the largest glacier in mainland Europe.[44]

Did You Know? Vestland is home to the Sognefjord, the "King of the Fjords," stretching over 200 kilometers and boasting awe-inspiring cliffs and cascading waterfalls.

Experiences:

Flåm Railway: Take a trip on the Flåm Railway, one of the steepest railways in the world. Wind through dramatic mountainscapes, witness cascading waterfalls and marvel at the engineering feat that is this iconic railway.

Hardangerfjord Fruit Route: Cycle or drive through the scenic Hardangerfjord Fruit Route, passing rolling hills dotted with orchards. Sample fresh berries and fruit wines, visit different farms and enjoy the breathtaking views of the fjord.

Jostedalsbreen Glacier Hike: Embark on a guided glacier hike on the majestic Jostedalsbreen, experiencing the raw power and icy beauty of this natural wonder firsthand. Learn about glacial formations, feel the crunch of ice under your boots, and create unforgettable memories amidst this awe-inspiring landscape.

Bergen International Festival: Immerse yourself in the vibrant energy of the Bergen International Festival, one of the world's oldest and largest music festivals. Enjoy diverse performances, from classical orchestras to contemporary music, dance, and theater, set against the backdrop of Bergen's historic streets.

Sognefjord RIB Boat Tour: Experience the thrill of a high-speed RIB (rigid inflatable boat) tour on the Sognefjord, skimming the water's surface and feeling the spray of the waves. Zip past towering cliffs, explore hidden coves, and get up close to waterfalls for a truly exhilarating adventure.

Trolltunga Hike: For the intrepid explorer, conquer the challenging hike to Trolltunga ("Troll Tongue"), a dramatic rock formation jutting out from a mountainside over 700 meters above the lake. Savor the stunning views and test your endurance on this unforgettable journey.

Fjords and Glaciers Kayak Tour: Explore the hidden corners of the fjords and get up close to glaciers on a guided kayak tour. Paddle through tranquil waters, witness calving glaciers firsthand, and experience the serenity of nature from a unique perspective.

Family Fun:

Vilvite Science Center: Spark your children's imaginations at the Vilvite Science Center in Bergen, an interactive playground for curious minds.

Explore exhibits on the human body, space, and technology, engage in hands-on experiments, and discover the wonders of science in a fun and engaging way.

Address: Thormohlens Gate 51, 5006 Bergen, Norway.

Akvariet I Bergen: Dive into the fascinating underwater world at Akvariet i Bergen, one of the largest aquariums in Scandinavia. Laugh at playful otters, marvel at majestic sharks, and learn about the diverse marine life found in the North Sea and beyond.

Address: Nordnesbakken 4, 5005 Bergen, Norway.

Flåm Railway: The scenic journey on the Flåm Railway is sure to captivate kids and adults alike. Watch waterfalls cascade down mountainsides, spot wildlife in the forests, and marvel at the engineering marvel of this iconic railway.

Address: 5743 Flam, Norway.

Viking Village: Step back in time at the Viking Village near Stavanger, where families can experience life in Viking times. Explore reconstructed houses, dress up in Viking attire, and participate in traditional activities like archery and axe throwing.

Address: Kong Augvalds veg 101, 4262 Avaldsnes, Norway.

Sognefjord Family Cruise: Choose a child-friendly cruise on the Sognefjord, offering pirate-themed adventures, face painting, and storytelling sessions while parents relax and enjoy the breathtaking scenery.

Did You Know? Composer Edvard Grieg, known for his evocative music inspired by Norwegian landscapes, was born and raised in Bergen and has left a lasting mark on the region's cultural identity.

Where to Eat:

Bryggen Tracteursted (Bergen): Savor traditional Norwegian fare with a modern twist at Bryggen Tracteursted, housed in a historic building on Bryggen Wharf. Indulge in fresh seafood, reindeer stew, and homemade desserts while enjoying the vibrant atmosphere of the harbor.

Address: Bryggestredet 2, 5003 Bergen, Norway.

Lysverket (Bergen): Experience Nordic cuisine focusing on fresh, seasonal ingredients at Lysverket, a Michelin-starred restaurant offering stunning city views. Sample artfully presented dishes, savor creative flavors, and treat yourself to a truly memorable dining experience.

Address: Rasmus Meyers alle 9, 5015 Bergen, Norway.

Garasjebryggeriet (Haugesund): Sample regional craft beers and delicious pub food at Garasjebryggeriet in Haugesund. Share plates of tapas, savor succulent burgers and unwind in a lively atmosphere with live music and friendly service.

Address: Smedasundet 66, 5528 Haugesund, Norway.

Shopping Guide:

Strandgaten (Bergen): This bustling street in Bergen's city center offers a mix of international brands and local shops. Browse for clothing, electronics, and souvenirs, or indulge in sweet treats at one of the cafes lining the street.

Address: Strandgaten, 5004 Bergen, Norway.

Fjordbutikken (Various Locations): Find a souvenir for everyone at Fjordbutikken, which has branches in several towns throughout Vestland. Choose from traditional Norwegian crafts, Viking-themed merchandise, and locally made delicacies, all with a hint of fjord magic.

Husfliden (Various Locations): Step into a world of traditional textiles and handicrafts at Husfliden, with retail outlets in Bergen, Ålesund, and other towns. Take home hand-knitted sweaters, woven blankets, and unique home items, all crafted with generations-old techniques and bearing the warmth of Norwegian heritage.

Entertainment:

Den Nationale Scene (Bergen): Den Nationale Scene is Norway's oldest theatre and a cultural landmark in Bergen. Enjoy dramas, comedies, and musicals staged in both classic and contemporary settings, offering a diverse and engaging experience.

Address: Engen 1, 5803 Bergen, Norway.

Grieghallen (Bergen): Buy tickets to world-class music performances at Grieghallen, a concert hall named after the renowned Norwegian composer Edvard Grieg. From classical orchestras to jazz concerts and folk music, there's something for every taste in this acoustically stunning venue.

Address: Edvard Griegs plass 1, 5015 Bergen, Norway.

Bergen Kino (Bergen): Catch the latest blockbusters or discover independent gems at Bergen Kino, a multi-screen cinema offering a variety of films throughout the year. Relax in comfortable seats, enjoy popcorn and refreshments, and lose yourself in the magic of the silver screen.

Address: Neumanns gate 3, 5015 Bergen, Norway.

FestspiLlene i Bergen (Bergen International Festival): FestspLllene i Bergen is one of the world's oldest and largest music festivals. Enjoy a mix of performances, from classical orchestras to contemporary music, dance, and theater, set against the backdrop of Bergen's historic streets.

Sports and Leisure:

Kayaking and Stand-Up Paddleboarding: Embrace the spirit of adventure by kayaking through the tranquil waters of the fjords or exploring hidden coves on a stand-up paddleboard. Rent a board, join a guided tour, or simply enjoy the serenity of gliding across the water surrounded by stunning scenery.

Glacier Climbing and Hiking: For the truly adventurous, tackle the challenge of glacier climbing and hiking on Jostedalsbreen, Europe's largest mainland glacier. Experience the icy grip of the ice, witness breathtaking crevasses, and conquer unforgettable peaks with the guidance of experienced instructors.

Whitewater Rafting: Get your adrenaline pumping with a whitewater rafting adventure on one of Vestland's wild rivers. Navigate rapids and experience the raw power of nature as you navigate turbulent waters surrounded by stunning scenery.

Accommodations:

Jostedalsbreen National Park: Immerse yourself in the pristine wilderness of Jostedalsbreen National Park by staying at one of the lodges there, which will offer you rustic yet comfortable accommodation and direct access to glacier hikes. Campsite options are also available for a truly immersive experience.

Vestland is just a gateway to the wonders of Norway. Head north to explore the vibrant city of Trondheim, delve into the Sami culture in Finnmark, or witness the Northern Lights illuminate the Arctic sky. With its towns, breathtaking landscapes, and endless adventure opportunities, Vestland promises an unforgettable journey that will leave you mesmerized by the magic of Norway.

Møre og Romsdal: Where Art Nouveau Flourishes

Møre og Romsdal, a name that rolls off the tongue like a Viking greeting, beckons you to a land where art and nature collide spectacularly. This region is splashed with green valleys that tumble into sapphire fjords, crowned by snow-capped peaks piercing the sky. It's the essence of Møre og Romsdal, a Norwegian county pulsating with breathtaking beauty and captivating history.

Historical Background:

Møre og Romsdal's history is etched in the rugged coastline and Viking sagas. Ancient burial mounds tell of seafaring prowess, while fishing villages like Ålesund bear witness to centuries of tradition. I⁰ the 19th century, a devastating fire transformed Ålesund, but from the ashes rose a phoenix of Art Nouveau architecture, earning it the moniker "the Nordic City of Jugendstil." Today, Møre og Romsdal celebrates its rich tapestry of Viking whispers, artistic vibrancy, and outdoor adventures, weaving an unforgettable story for modern travelers.

Main Attractions:

Ålesund: Immerse yourself in the architectural fairytale of Ålesund. Wander through streets lined with colorful Art Nouveau buildings, their facades adorned with whimsical curves and floral motifs. Explore the Jugendstilsenteret museum, climb Aksla mountain for panoramic city views, and savor fresh seafood at the bustling fish market.

As of the writing of this book, the normal opening hours for the Jugendstilsenteret Museum are every day from 10 am to 5 pm. You can also visit Aksla mountain at any time during your trip. However, please always double-check the opening hours online should there have been any slight change in their schedule.

Jugendstilsenteret Museum Address: Apotekergata 16, 6004 Alesund, Norway.

Immerse yourself in the architectural fairytale of Ålesund.[45]

Geirangerfjord: Embark on a journey through the UNESCO-listed Geirangerfjord, a masterpiece of nature carved by ancient glaciers. Cruise past cascading waterfalls, towering cliffs, and villages nestled amidst the dramatic scenery. Witness the Seven Sisters waterfall cascading down the mountainside, a spectacle that will leave you speechless.

As of the writing of this book, the normal opening hours are daily from 9 am till 7 pm, but please always double-check the opening hours online should there have been any slight change in their schedule.

Embark on a journey through the UNESCO-listed Geirangerfjord, a masterpiece of nature carved by ancient glaciers.[46]

Trollstigen: Feel the thrill of winding up the serpentine Trollstigen, a road so dramatic it seems ripped straight from a mythological tale. Navigate hairpin bends, marvel at cascading waterfalls, and see the stunning panorama from the viewing platforms, all while experiencing the engineering marvel of this iconic road.

Feel the thrill of winding up the serpentine Trollstigen, a road so dramatic it seems ripped straight from a mythological tale.[47]

Romsdalseggen Ridge: Lace up your hiking boots and conquer the Romsdalseggen Ridge, a 10-kilometer trek showcasing Møre og Romsdal's most breathtaking panorama. Hike through alpine meadows, traverse dramatic peaks and admire breathtaking views of the Trolltindane peaks and valleys below.

Lace up your hiking boots and conquer the Romsdalseggen Ridge, a 10-kilometer trek showcasing Møre og Romsdal's most breathtaking panorama.[48]

The Atlantic Road: Drive along the scenic Atlantic Road, an 8.3-kilometer stretch of road weaving across small islands and bridges, offering stunning sea views and a unique driving experience.

Drive along the scenic Atlantic Road, an 8.3-kilometer stretch of road weaving across small islands and bridges, offering stunning sea views and a unique driving experience.[49]

Transport:

Møre og Romsdal is a large and diverse county with a variety of transport options available to travelers. The main airport in the region is Ålesund Airport, Vigra (AES), which offers international and domestic flights. There are also several smaller airports in the region, including Molde Airport, Årø (MOL), Kristiansund Airport, Kvernberget (KSU), and Ørsta-Volda Airport, Hovden (HOV).

Public transportation within the region is efficient and affordable. A network of buses and ferries connects major towns and villages. The Hurtigruten coastal express ship also makes a stop in Ålesund, allowing travelers to embark on a breathtaking journey along the Norwegian coast.

If you plan on exploring the region by car, a network of scenic roads crisscross the county. The Atlantic Road, Trollstigen, and Romsdalseggen Ridge are just a few routes offering stunning views of the fjords, mountains, and coastline.

Experiences:

Geiranger Skywalk: Test your bravery on the Geiranger Skywalk, a glass platform extending 32 meters overlooking the Geirangerfjord. Gaze down at the breathtaking scenery below, feel the wind whipping through your hair, and create unforgettable memories of this thrilling experience.

Address: Dalsnibba, Nibbevegen 451, 6216 Geiranger, Norway.

Romsdalseggen Hike with Guide: Conquer the challenging Romsdalseggen Ridge with the guidance of an experienced local guide. Learn about the local flora and fauna, navigate safely through rocky terrain, and savor the accomplishment of reaching the summit.

Ålesund Food Tour: Embark on a culinary journey through Ålesund, savoring the bounty of the sea and the land. Visit local restaurants, cafes, and hidden gems, sampling traditional dishes like fresh seafood, cured meats, and homemade cheeses. Learn about the region's culinary heritage, meet passionate producers, and indulge in unique flavors that will tantalize your taste buds.

Did You Know? Møre og Romsdal boasts the most peaks exceeding 2000 meters in Norway, making it a paradise for mountaineering enthusiasts.

Family Fun:

AIvariet I Ålesund: Visit the fascinating underwater world at Ikvariet i Ålesund, one of the largest aquariums in Scandinavia. Encounter playful otters, marvel at majestic sharks, and learn about the diverse marine life found in the North Sea and beyond. Children will be mesmerized by the colorful exhibits and interactive displays, making it a perfect educational and entertaining outing.

Address: Tuenesvegen 200, 6006 Ålesund, Norway.

Romsdal Museum: Step back in time at the Romsdal Museum, where families can explore the history and culture of the region. Learn about Viking traditions, see traditional costumes and tools, and participate in hands-on activities that bring the past to life. Kids will love the interactive exhibits and the historical buildings, making it a fun and educational experience for all ages.

Address: Per Amdams veg 4, 6413 Molde, Norway.

Trollstigen Visitor Center: Make a pit stop at the Trollstigen Visitor Center before conquering the iconic road. Children will be captivated by the interactive exhibits showcasing the engineering feat of the road, the power of nature, and the local folklore. Enjoy panoramic views from the viewing platform, grab a refreshing snack, and get ready for the thrilling drive ahead.

Address: Istrdalsvegen 1515, 6300 Andalsnes, Norway.

Geirangerfjord Cruise: Embark on a family-friendly cruise through the majestic Geirangerfjord. Spot waterfalls cascading down the cliffs, keep an eye out for dolphins and porpoises and learn about the geological wonders of the fjord. Many cruises offer children's activities and storytelling sessions, making it an enjoyable experience for the whole family.

Hjørundfjord Hiking: Explore Hjørundfjord on a family-friendly hike. Choose a trail suitable for all ages, soak in the breathtaking scenery of towering mountains and emerald waters, and enjoy a picnic lunch amidst the serene nature. It's a perfect way to connect with nature and create lasting memories.

Where to Eat:

Brasserie Posten: Experience panoramic fjord views and delectable dishes at Brassie Posten, a restaurant overlooking Geirangerfjord. Indulge in delicious food made with local Norwgian produce.

Address: Geitangervegen 4, 6216 Geiranger, Norway.

Trollstigen Kafé: Refuel after conquering Trollstigen at the Trollstigen Kafé, a cozy cafeteria offering traditional Norwegian fare. Warm up with a hot coffee and a slice of homemade cake, sample hearty meatballs, and enjoy the views of the dramatic Trollstigen road.

Address: Trollstigen, 6300 Andalsnes, Norway.

Shopping Guide:

Ålesund Storsenter: Located in the heart of Ålesund, Ålesund Storsenter houses stores for you to visit and shop from. It also has a variety of restaurants and cafes and is not far from other locations you may want to visit in Ålesund.

Address: Grimmergata 1, 6002 Ålesund, Norway.

The Harbour Gift Shop: Discover locally made crafts and artwork at Alnes Brygge, a store near the harbor in Ålesund. Find unique souvenir home decor items, clothing, toys, and local food, making it a perfect place to pick up a memento of your trip.

Address: Lorkenesgata 1, 6002 Ålesund, Norway.

E Merok Turisthandel AS: Stock up on Geirangerfjord-themed souvenirs at the E Merok Turisthandel AS, offering everything from postcards and magnets to Viking helmets and trolls. Find something for everyone at this convenient location before your departure.

Address: Ornevegen 2, 6216 Geiranger, Norway.

Entertainment:

Aalesund Museum (Ålesund): Delve into the fascinating history and culture of Ålesund at the Aalesund Museum. Explore exhibits of the town's beautiful Art Nouveau architecture, learn about traditional fishing practices, and discover the secrets of this coastal city.

Address: Rasmus Ronnebergs gate 16, 6002 Alesund, Norway.

Accommodations:

Ålesund: Embrace the Art Nouveau architecture of Ålesund by staying at the Hotel Brosundet, housed in a historic waterfront building. Budget travelers can find comfortable options at hostels and guesthouses in the town center. Campers will find scenic campsites overlooking the water, offering an unforgettable experience under the midnight sun.

Hotel Brosundet Address: Apotekergata 1, 5, 6004 Alesund, Norway.

Geirangerfjord: Experience fjord serenity at waterfront hotels or lodges. The Union Geiranger Hotel & Spa offers luxury, while Grande Hytteutleie og Camping provides cozy cabins for families or groups.

The Union Geiranger Hotel & Spa Address: Geirangervegen 100, 6216 Geiranger, Norway.

Grande Hytteutleie og Camping Address: Ornevegen 190, 6216 Geiranger, Norway.

The Atlantic Road: Stay at seaside hotels or guesthouses along the road, offering direct access to the dramatic scenery and the power of the ocean storms.

Romsdalseggen Ridge: Hikers seeking immersion can stay at a mountain lodge with basic comfort and direct access to the trail. Campsite options are also available for experienced hikers.

The Outer Islands: Discover the charm of these islands by staying in local guesthouses or renting cabins, offering a truly authentic experience.

Remember, this is just a starting point for your Møre og Romsdal adventure. With its endless opportunities for exploration, breathtaking scenery, and captivating history, this region is sure to leave you mesmerized and yearning for more.

As your Western Norwegian adventure reaches its end, the memories you carry will resonate like the echoes of a folk song, each one a treasured verse in the poem of your journey. You'll recall the sun-kissed fjords shimmering under twilight, the taste of fresh seafood plucked from the ocean, and the thrill of conquering a rugged mountain path. You'll remember the stories whispered by waterfalls, the warmth of local smiles, and the sense of belonging you felt amidst the grandeur of this ancient land.

Chapter 7: Central Norway (Trøndelag)

Venture beyond the iconic southern fjords and discover a less-trodden yet equally breathtaking Norway. Here in Trøndelag, Central Norway's crown jewel, emerald waters carve through landscapes of verdant valleys and rolling hills, creating a canvas of natural splendor unlike any other. From jagged peaks piercing the sky to secluded coves whispering secrets of the sea, Trøndelag offers a symphony of nature's finest compositions, waiting to be discovered.

Trøndelag.[50]

Whether you're a seasoned adventurer seeking epic hikes and thrilling whitewater rafting, a casual explorer longing for fjordside serenity, or a culture enthusiast drawn to Viking whispers and vibrant cities, Trøndelag welcomes you with open arms and promises an unforgettable Norwegian experience.

Historical Background

Trøndelag's past is etched into the landscape. Viking sagas whisper from burial mounds scattered across the valleys while imposing stone fortresses stand as silent sentinels of turbulent times. In Trondheim, the magnificent Nidaros Cathedral, a Gothic masterpiece, boasts a legacy as the coronation church for Norwegian monarchs. The town of Røros, a UNESCO World Heritage Site, is a monument to the tales of miners who toiled beneath the earth, extracting copper that fueled Norway's rise. From the bustling trade routes of the past to the pioneering spirit of modern explorers like Roald Amundsen, Trøndelag's rich tapestry of history continues to inspire and captivate.

Main Attractions

Trondheim: Immerse yourself in the vibrant heart of Trøndelag. Explore the majestic Nidaros Cathedral, a Gothic masterpiece, and wander through the Bakklandet district, lined with colorful wooden houses. Discover Viking history at Sverresborg Trondelag Folk Museum or climb Kristiansten Fortress for panoramic views. Savor the city's cultural scene at the Rockheim Museum.

As of the writing of this book, the opening hours for the Sverresborg Trondelag Folk Museum are Saturday to Wednesday from 10 am to 5 pm and Thursday and Friday from 10 am to pm. The opening hours for the Kristiansten Fortress are Monday to Saturday from 10 am to 4 pm and Sunday from 12 pm to 4 pm. The opening hours for the Rockheim Museum are Tuesday to Friday from 10 am to 4 pm, Saturday and Sunday from 11 am to 5 pm, and closed on Monday. However, please always double-check the opening hours online should there have been any slight change in their schedule.

Sverresborg Trondelag Folk Museum Address: Sverresborg Alle 13, 7020 Trondheim, Norway.

Kristiansten Fortress Address: Kristiantensbakken 60, 7014 Trondheim, Norway.

Rockheim Museum Address: Brattørkaia 14, 7010 Trondheim, Norway.

Explore the majestic Nidaros Cathedral, a Gothic masterpiece, and wander through the Bakklandet district, lined with colorful wooden houses.[51]

Røros: Step back in time to this UNESCO World Heritage Site. Explore the wooden houses adorned with red paint, wander the cobbled streets, and soak in the authentic atmosphere. Visit the Rørosmuseet to learn about the town's mining past or enjoy a traditional meal.

As of the writing of this book, you can visit Røros at any time during your trip. The opening hours for the Rørosmuseet are every day from 10 am to 4 pm.However, please always double-check the opening hours online should there have been any slight change in their schedule.

Rørosmuseet Address: Lorentz Lossius Gata 45, 7374 Røros, Norway.

Explore the wooden houses adorned with red paint, wander the cobbled streets, and soak in the authentic atmosphere.[52]

Fjords: Embark on a fjord cruise and witness the grandeur of nature. Marvel at the UNESCO-listed Geirangerfjord and Nærøyfjord, known for their waterfalls, towering cliffs, and tranquil beauty. Kayak in the serene Trondheim Fjord or hike alongside the majestic Sognefjord, where waterfalls tumble into emerald valleys.

Marvel at the UNESCO-listed Geirangerfjord and Nærøyfjord, known for their waterfalls, towering cliffs, and tranquil beauty.[53]

Munkholmen: Discover the secrets of this mysterious island in Trondheim Fjord. Explore the ruins of the medieval monastery, climb the historic Munkholmen Fortress, and soak in the breathtaking fjord views. Imagine the whispers of monks chanting prayers centuries ago or the tales of prisoners held within the fort's walls.

As of the writing of this book, the opening hours for the Munkholmen Fortess are every day from 11 am to 4 pm, but please always double-check the opening hours online should there be any slight changes in their schedule.

Munkholmen Fortress Address: Frostaveien 2, 7043 Trondheim, Norway.

Discover the secrets of this mysterious island in Trondheim Fjord.[54]

Kristiansund and Averøy Island: Extend your adventure in the coastal town of Kristiansund, where colorful houses huddle on the edge of the sea, or venture to the quaint fishing village of Bud, its harbor alive with the rhythmic bobbing of boats. Breathe in the salty air on Averøy Island, where hidden beaches beckon with promises of sun-kissed relaxation and dramatic cliff walks.

As of the writing of this book, the normal opening hours daily are all 24 hours of the day, but please always double-check the opening hours online should there have been any slight change in their schedule.

Extend your adventure in the coastal town of Kristiansund, where colorful houses huddle on the edge of the sea.[55]

Did You Know? The Nidelva River, a vital artery of Trondheim, was once known as the "Salmon River" due to the abundance of these majestic fish that once graced its waters. Today, dedicated conservation efforts are restoring salmon populations, promising a glimpse into the river's glorious past.

Beyond the Tourist Trail

While the well-trodden paths of Trondheim and Røros offer undeniable charm, Trøndelag whispers secrets to those who venture beyond the typical tourist trail.

Island Hopping in the Trøndelag Coast: Unveil the soul of the islands. Sail to hidden coves on Hitra, where puffins nest on rugged cliffs, explore the quaint fishing village of Kråkesøyer, and sample fresh seafood delicacies in bustling Kristiansund. Kayak amidst the kelp forests of Smøla, renowned for its unique marine life, or climb the majestic peak of Storheia for panoramic views of the archipelago.

Sámi Culture in Snåsa: Immerse yourself in the ancient wisdom of the Sámi people, Norway's indigenous community. Visit the Snåsa Sámi Siida and learn about their rich traditions, from reindeer herding and yoik (joik) singing to their intricate handcrafts. Experience the thrill of a reindeer sledding tour across snow-dusted plains or savor a traditional meal in a Sámi lavvo tent, listening to captivating stories by firelight.

Glacier Hiking in Jotunheimen National Park: Hike through breathtaking valleys carved by glaciers, leaving footprints in the snow alongside the tracks of Arctic foxes. Scale Galdh'piggen, Norway's highest peak, and stand on the roof of the country, basking in the panorama of endless mountain ranges. Camp under the canvas of a star-studded sky, feeling the silence of the mountains resonate in your soul.

Cycling the Pilgrim's Route: Embrace the spirit of pilgrimage on two wheels. Follow the historic route from Trondheim to Nidaros Cathedral, a journey undertaken by devout travelers for centuries. Cycle through picturesque villages, pause at ancient stave churches and savor the serene beauty of the Trondheim Fjord. Breath in the region's rich spiritual heritage.

Experiences

Trøndelag's tapestry of experiences offers threads for every traveler's desire.

Foodie Adventures: Discover the heart of culinary delights. Embark on a seafood odyssey in coastal villages, savoring succulent oysters plucked straight from the sea. Learn the secrets of baking Trøndersodd, a hearty lamb soup that warms the soul, or visit traditional farms and indulge in homemade cheeses and jams. Attend a lively food festival in Trondheim, where local chefs showcase their innovative takes on regional specialties.

Festivals and Events: Join the vibrant tapestry of celebrations. Witness the dazzling fireworks of St. Olav's Day, illuminating the Trondheim skyline, or participate in the Rørosmartnan, a centuries-old market fair teeming with traditional crafts and live music. Immerse yourself in the sounds of the Trondheim Jazz Festival or dance the night away at the Pstereo music festival, where emerging artists take center stage.

Hiking and Outdoor Activities: Let nature be your playground. Trek through fairytale forests adorned with moss and lichen, following cascading waterfalls to glacial lakes. Climb jagged peaks in Dovrefjell National Park, where musk oxen roam the tundra, or kayak through the mirror-like waters of Geirangerfjord, flanked by towering cliffs. For the adrenaline-seekers, white-water rafting on the Sjoa River provides exhilarating thrills, while snowmobiling across frozen landscapes offers an arctic adventure unparalleled.

Cultural Discoveries: Unearth historical treasures and traditions. Visit Nidaros Cathedral, a Gothic masterpiece, and marvel at its stained-glass windows and ancient tombs. Explore the vibrant Rockheim museum, delving into the history of Norwegian music, or the Viking past at the Sverresborg fortress, where battles echo through the stone walls. Learn about Sámi reindeer herding practices at the Snåsa Sámi Siida, or discover the unique Røros copper mine, a UNESCO World Heritage Site, its tunnels whispering tales of miners and their toil.

Did You Know? Trondheim's vibrant Bakklandet district, once a haven for artisans and fishermen, is now a trendy hub for cafes, galleries, and independent shops, offering a delightful contrast between historic charm and modern flair.

Family Fun

Trøndelag offers a playground where laughter blends with wonder, creating memories that will last a lifetime.

Trondheim Science Center: Ignite young minds with interactive exhibits. Journey through the human body, explore the mysteries of space, and witness thrilling science demonstrations. Let curiosity take flight in the planetarium or build robots in the workshop, transforming imagination into reality.

Address: Kongens gate 1, 7011 Trondheim, Norway.

Graakallbanen (Trondheim Tramway): Embark on an adventure on a funicular railway. Ride the vintage tram from St. Olav's Gate and enjoy more sights of the city with your children and see the beautiful lake and the end of the line at Lian. Fortunately, you can also swim in the lake if the weather permits.

Trondheim Bymark: Hike through a fairytale forest. Escape the city bustle and explore the enchanting Trondheim Bymark, a sprawling forest just a stone's throw from the city center. Follow winding trails through pine and birch groves, encounter playful red squirrels, and breathe in the fresh forest air. Pack a picnic and find a sun-dappled clearing to enjoy a cozy lunch surrounded by nature's beauty.

Address: Trondheim, Norway.

NTNU Science Museum: Spark your curiosity at the NTNU Science Museum, where interactive exhibits bring science to life. Children can explore the human body through giant models, delve into the secrets of the universe in the planetarium, and witness captivating live experiments. This educational adventure will leave young minds buzzing with questions and a newfound appreciation for the wonders of the world.

Address: Erling Skakkes gate 47B, 7012 Trondheim, Norway.

Where to Eat

Trøndelag's culinary scene caters to every palate, from adventurous foodies to families seeking kid-friendly fare.

Troll Restaurant: Savor waterfront dining with a view. Indulge in a fine dining experience at Troll Restaurant, with a view of the Nidelva River. Enjoy a delicious three-course or five-coures meal, depending on your preference, made with the freshest ingredients and the highest quality.

Address: Fosenkaia 4A, 7010 Trondheim, Norway.

Baklandet Bakeries: Treat your taste buds to sweet delights. Wander through the streets of Bakklandet and discover an array of enticing bakeries, each exuding mouthwatering aromas. Pick up a warm and gooey cinnamon bun, indulge in a traditional Trønderslefse (potato flatbread) slathered with brunost (brown cheese), or savor a freshly baked croissant with a steaming cup of coffee.

Ravnkloa: Grab a quick and delicious bite on the go. Located in the heart of Trondheim, Ravnkloa is a bustling food market offering a global smorgasbord of culinary delights. Choose from fresh sushi bowls, steaming bao buns, Italian pizzas, or spicy Thai curries. Find a sunny spot on the outdoor terrace and enjoy the lively atmosphere while devouring your delicious Ieal.

Grano Trondheim: Savor Italian cuisine at Grano Trondheim, serving authentic Italian dishes including, pizzas, pasta, paninis, and desserts. Enjoy the cozy seating and delicious food with a wonderful view.

Address: Sondre gate 25, 7010 Trondheim, Norway.

Shopping Guide

From souvenirs that whisper of Viking sagas to handcrafted treasures passed down through generations, Trøndelag offers a shopper's paradise.

Røros Shops: Lose yourself in a world of wooden wonders. Step into the wooden houses of Røros and discover a treasure trove of traditional crafts. Admire beautifully woven Røros-textiles, browse intricately carved wooden bowls and figurines, and pick up a unique souvenir that embodies the spirit of this historic town.

Ravnkloa Fiskehaller: Dive into the bounty of the sea. Immerse yourself in the atmosphere of the Ravnkloa Fiskehaller, where colorful stalls display the freshest catches of the day. Sample succulent oysters plucked straight from the fjord, pick up smoked salmon to take home as a delicacy, or choose from a variety of fish, ready to be grilled or poached to perfection.

Bakklandet Art and Design Shops: Unearth creative gems. Unwind and wander through the streets of Bakklandet, where local artists and designers showcase their talents in independent shops and galleries. Discover unique jewelry crafted from recycled materials, admire paintings capturing the region's breathtaking landscapes, or find the perfect handmade souvenir to remind you of your Trøndelag adventure.

Trondheim Torg: Trondheim Tord is a bustling shopping mall at the heart of Trondheim. This shopping center has a variety of stores, offering clothes, shoes, home goods, and more. There are also a variety of restaurants and cafes to enjoy.

Address: Kongens gate 9, 7013 Trondheim, Norway.

Did You Know? The Atlantic Road, a breathtaking engineering marvel, was built against all odds, withstanding the fury of the Atlantic Ocean to connect remote island communities. This "road to nowhere" symbolizes Norwegian resilience and is a must-drive for any adventurous spirit.

Entertainment

Whether you crave lively nightlife or intimate cultural experiences, Trøndelag's entertainment scene has something for everyone.

Nidaros Cathedral Concerts: Immerse yourself in the harmonious sounds of sacred music. Attend a classical concert held within the majestic Nidaros Cathedral, where the Gothic architecture and stained-glass windows create a breathtaking backdrop for choral performances and renowned organ recitals. Experience the spiritual power of music as it soars through the cathedral's vaulted ceilings, leaving you feeling uplifted and inspired.

Address: Kongsgardsgata 2, 7013 Trondheim, Norway,

Rockheim Museum: Rock out to the rhythm of Norwegian music. Uncover the history of Norwegian music at the Rockheim Museum, an interactive and engaging experience. Explore exhibits showcasing iconic artists and instruments, relive legendary concerts through immersive simulations, and even try your hand at playing guitar or drums. Be swept away by the energy and passion of Norwegian music, from traditional folk tunes to electrifying contemporary bands.

Address: Brattorkaia 14, 7010 Trondheim, Norway.

Trondheim Symphony Orchestra: Immerse yourself in the world of classical music. For a truly grand musical experience, attend a performance by the Trondheim Symphony Orchestra, one of Norway's leading ensembles. Witness the skill and passion of talented musicians as they bring to life the works of classical masters and contemporary composers. Let the music wash over you as you sit in the historic Trondheim Concert Hall, a stunning venue with ornate decoration and excellent acoustics.

Sports and Leisure

Trøndelag's breathtaking landscapes and vibrant spirit ignite a sense of adventure in every soul. Whether you're a seasoned athlete seeking adrenaline-pumping thrills or a relaxed soul yearning for peaceful pursuits, this region offers a playground for every passion.

For the Thrill Seekers:

Conquer the Fjords: Kayak through the serene waters of the Geirangerfjord or kayak alongside humpback whales in the Trondheim Fjord. Ride the rapids of the Sjoa River on a white-water rafting adventure, or test your climbing skills on the challenging cliffs of Romsdalen.

Embrace the Snow: Shred the slopes of Oppdal or Røros, renowned for their powdery snow and stunning mountain vistas. Go dogsledding across frozen landscapes, chase the Northern Lights on a snowmobile safari, or try your hand at ice climbing on frozen waterfalls.

Hit the Trails: Hike through pristine valleys and conquer snow-capped peaks in Jotunheimen National Park. Cycle scenic routes along the Trondheim Fjord or challenge yourself on the demanding Trondheim-Oslo bike route.

For the Relaxation Seekers:

Sail the Seas: Embark on a leisurely cruise through the archipelago, stopping to explore islands like Hitra and Smøla. Cast your line for salmon in crystal-clear rivers, or simply soak up the sun on a secluded beach.

Find Your Zen: Unwind in a traditional Norwegian sauna, enveloped by warmth and rejuvenating steam. Breathe in the fresh mountain air on a leisurely hike or find your inner peace amidst the serene beauty of a fjord.

Embrace the Culture: Immerse yourself in the vibrant culture of Trondheim, visiting museums like the Rockheim or Nidaros Cathedral.

Explore the wooden houses of Røros or attend a traditional Sámi festival in Snåsa.

Family Fun:

Splash Around: Make a splash at the largest water park in the region, or enjoy hours of fun at the Trondheim Bymark recreation area. Build sandcastles on the beach, go on a family bike ride, or explore the fascinating exhibits at the NTNU Science Museum.

Treasure Hunt: Embark on a scavenger hunt through Trondheim, following clues and discovering hidden gems.

Go Fishing: Bond with your family over a fishing trip on a tranquil lake or the mighty Trondheim Fjord. Learn the art of fly fishing, cook your catch over a campfire, and create memories that will last a lifetime.

Accommodations

Trøndelag's diverse landscapes and vibrant spirit demand a diverse accommodation scene. From mountain cabins nestled in snowdrifts to modern hotels overlooking the fjords, there's something for every budget and preference. So, let's unlock your perfect Trøndelag haven:

For the Luxury Seekers:

Boutique Hotels: Immerse yourself in sophisticated charm in Trondheim's heart. Enjoy panoramic city views, pampering spa treatments, and gourmet dining at hotels like Clarion Hotel Trondheim or Britannia Hotel. Wake up to the gentle lapping of the Nidelva River and feel the pulse of the city from your luxurious haven.

Clarion Hotel Trondheim Address: Brattørkaia 1, 7010 Trondheim, Norway.

Britannia Hotel Address: Dronningens gate 5, 7011 Trondheim, Norway.

Glamping Escapes: Elevate your camping experience in the wilds of Trøndelag. Glamping sites offer stylish and comfortable tents with all the amenities, from plush beds and hot tubs to private terraces overlooking breathtaking scenery. Imagine gazing at the Northern Lights from your cozy cocoon under the vast arctic sky.

For the Budget-Conscious:

Charming Guesthouses: Discover the warmth of local hospitality in smaller towns and villages. In villages like Røros and Bud, guesthouses like Finnegarden Røros offer comfortable and affordable rooms, often decorated with traditional touches. Enjoy delicious homemade breakfasts, chat with friendly locals, and experience the authentic charm of Trøndelag.

Finnegarden Røros Address: Bergmannsgata 11, 7374 Røros, Norway.

Camping and Hostels: Get back to nature and connect with fellow travelers. Campgrounds like Granmo Camping in Oppdal and hostels like Trondheim Vandrerhjem offer budget-friendly options for those who embrace a simple lifestyle. Pitch your tent under the midnight sun, cook meals over a campfire, and share stories with fellow adventurers under the starry sky.

Granmo Camping Address: Granmo Camping, Dovrevegen 638, 7340 Oppdal, Norway.

Trondheim Vandrerhjem Address: Weidemanns v. 41 B, 7043 Trondheim, Norway.

For the Nature Enthusiasts:

Mountain Cabins: Embrace the spirit of Norwegian "hygge" in a rustic cabin. Nestled amidst snow-capped peaks or on the shores of tranquil lakes, cabins like Femund Hytter offer cozy retreats for nature lovers. Hike to your doorstep, curl up by the fireplace with a good book, and wake up to the symphony of birdsong and rustling leaves.

Address: Utsikten 7, 2440 Engerdal, Norway.

Fishing Lodges: Cast your line and unwind in idyllic waterfront havens. Traditional fishing lodges like Storfjord Lodge offer comfortable accommodations, expert guidance for avid anglers, and access to some of Norway's most productive fishing grounds. Savor fresh seafood feasts, breathe in the salty air, and let the rhythm of the waves lull you to sleep.

Address: Ovre Glomset 110, 6260 Skodje, Norway.

For the Family:

Family-Friendly Hotels: Create lasting memories with your loved ones. Choose hotels like Scandic Nidelven or Thon Hotel Nidaros in Trondheim, offering spacious rooms, dedicated play areas, and kid-friendly amenities. Let children loose in indoor water parks, enjoy movie nights and family-themed buffets, and create unforgettable moments with game nights and scavenger hunts.

Scandic Nidelven Address: Havnegata 1-3, 7010 Trondheim, Norway.

Thon Hotel Nidaros Address: Sondre gate 22B, 7010 Trondheim, Norway.

Vacation Homes: Gather your family in a spacious and welcoming home away from home. Renting a vacation home provides privacy, flexibility, and ample space for family gatherings. Cook meals together, play board games by the fireplace, and enjoy the freedom of exploring Trøndelag at your own pace.

As you depart from Trøndelag, the lingering memory of rolling hills cascading into a fjord will stay with you like a cherished talisman. The echoes of Viking sagas whispered through ancient ruins, the thrill of conquering dramatic peaks, and the quietude of pristine lakes reflecting the starlit sky are the treasures you carry home. This region is an invitation to embrace the simple beauty of nature, connect with the rich cultural tapestry, and forge a connection with the land that resonates long after you bid farewell.

Chapter 8: Northern Norway (Nord-Norge)

As you journey north, Norway sheds its emerald cloak and dons a dazzling garment of snow and ice. Welcome to Nord-Norge, the final chapter in your exploration of this captivating land. Here, the Arctic whispers against the granite cliffs, and the sun plays peek-a-boo with the horizon. Prepare to be captivated by soaring mountains scraping the twilight sky and a coastline carved into a thousand mesmerizing islands. Nord-Norge is a medley of breathtaking vistas, vibrant Sámi culture, and echoes of a rich and sometimes turbulent history.

Nord-Norge.[56]

Troms og Finnmark: Your Guide to Norway's Arctic Wonderland

Troms og Finnmark, Norway's northernmost region, is a land of breathtaking beauty, rich culture, and endless adventure. This Arctic wonderland offers something for everyone, from the vibrant city of Tromsø to the remote villages of Finnmark. Whether you're chasing the Northern Lights, skiing under the midnight sun, or learning about the Sami people's fascinating way of life, Troms og Finnmark is sure to leave you speechless.

Historical Background

Troms og Finnmark has been inhabited for centuries by the Sami people, who have adapted their lives to the harsh Arctic climate. The region was also home to Viking settlements and later became a center for fur trade and fishing. In the 19th century, Tromsø emerged as a major port city, thanks to its strategic location on the Arctic Ocean. Today, Troms og Finnmark is a thriving region with a modern economy based on tourism, fishing, and petroleum.

Main Attractions

Tromsø: The largest city in Troms og Finnmark, Tromsø, is known as the "Gateway to the Arctic." Be sure to visit the Polar Museum, the Arctic Cathedral, the Fjellheisen cable car, and Kvaløya Island.

As of the writing of this book, the opening hours for the locations mentioned are as follows:

- **Polar Museum:** Every day from 11 am to 5 pm.
- **Arctic Cathedral:** Monday to Saturday from 9 am to 6 pm, Sunday from 1 pm to 6 pm.
- **Fjellheisen Cable Car:** Every day from 9 am to 12 am.
- **Kvaløya Island:** Every day at any time.

However, please make sure to double-check the opening hours online should there be any slight changes in their schedules.

Polar Museum Address: Sondre Trollbodgate 11B, 9008 Tromsø, Norway.

Arctic Cathedral Address: Hans Nilsens veg 41, 9020 Tromsdalen, Norway.

Fjellheisen Cable Car Address: Sollivegen 12, 9020 Tromsdalen, Norway.

Kvaløya Island Address: Tromsø, Norway.

The largest city in Troms og Finnmark, Tromsø, is known as the "Gateway to the Arctic." [57]

Alta: The northernmost city in the world, Alta is home to the Alta Museum (UNESCO World Heritage Site), the Northern Lights Cathedral, Alta Canyon, and Altafjord.

As of the writing of this book, the opening hours for the locations mentioned are as follows:

- **Alta Museum:** Every day from 9 am to 5 pm.
- **Northen Lights Cathedral:** Monday to Friday from 10 am to 2 pm, closed Saturday and Sunday.
- **Alta Canyon:** Every day at any time
- **Altafjord:** Every day at any time.

However, please make sure to double-check the opening hours online should there be any slight changes in their schedules.

Alta Museum Address: Altaveien 19, 9512 Alta, Norway.

Northern Lights Cathedral Address: Markedsgata 30, 9510 Alta, Norway.

Alta Canyon Address: 9518 Alta, Norway.

The northernmost city in the world, Alta is home to the Alta Museum (UNESCO World Heritage Site), the Northern Lights Cathedral, Alta Canyon, and Altafjord.[58]

Senja Island: The second largest island in Norway, Senja Island is a paradise for hikers, kayakers, and birdwatchers. Check out the stunning Husøy, Senjahopen, and Ersfjordbotn.

As of the writing of this book, the normal opening hours daily are all 24 hours of the day, but please always double-check the opening hours online should there have been any slight change in their schedule.

The second largest island in Norway, Senja Island is a paradise for hikers, kayakers, and birdwatchers.[59]

Finnmark Plateau: The homeland of the Sami people, the Finnmark Plateau is a great place to learn about Sami culture and experience traditional activities like skiing, snowmobiling, and dog sledding. Visit Kautokeino and Karasjok for authentic experiences.

As of the writing of this book, you can visit Kautokeino and Karasjok at any time during your visit. However, it is best to double-check should there be any changes.

The homeland of the Sami people, the Finnmark Plateau is a great place to learn about Sami culture and experience traditional activities.[60]

Nordkapp (North Cape): The northernmost point in continental Europe, Nordkapp is a must-see for any visitor to Troms og Finnmark. Visit the North Cape Hall (Nordkapphallen) for stunning views of the Arctic Ocean.

As of the writing of this book, the normal opening hours for the North Cape Hall are daily from 11 am till 1 am, but please always double-check the opening hours online should there have been any slight change in their schedule.

Visit the North Cape Hall (Nordkapphallen) for stunning views of the Arctic Ocean.[61]

Hammerfest: The world's northernmost town, Hammerfest is home to the Royal and Ancient Polar Bear Society and the Meridian Column.

The world's northernmost town, Hammerfest, is home to the Royal and Ancient Polar Bear Society.[62]

Did You Know? Mack Brewery is the world's northernmost brewery, and it's found in Tromsø.

Transport

Getting around Troms og Finnmark is easy, with a variety of transportation options available. The region is well-served by air, with airports in Tromsø, Alta, and Kirkenes. There is also a regular ferry service between Tromsø and mainland Norway. Once you're in Troms og Finnmark, you can get around by bus, train, or car.

Experiences

Northern Lights Chasing: Troms og Finnmark is one of the best places in the world to see the Northern Lights. Many companies offer guided Northern Lights tours, or you can try your luck spotting them on your own.

Midnight Sun: In the summer, the sun never sets in Troms og Finnmark. This makes it a great time to enjoy outdoor activities like hiking, biking, and fishing.

Sami Culture: The Sami people have a rich culture and history displayed in Troms og Finnmark. Visit a Sami village, try some traditional Sami food, and learn about their unique way of life.

Whale Watching: The waters off the coast of Troms og Finnmark are home to various whales, including humpback whales, minke whales, and orcas. There are many whale-watching tours available from Tromsø and Skjervøy.

Fishing: Troms og Finnmark is a paradise for anglers. The region is home to some of the world's best fishing for salmon, cod, and halibut.

Family Fun

Troms og Finnmark is a great place for families to visit. There are plenty of activities to keep kids entertained, from visiting the Polar Zoo in Tromsø to riding the Tromsø Cable Car. Families can enjoy snowmobiling, skiing, and dog sledding in the winter.

Polar Park Address: Bonesveien 319, 9360 Bardu, Norway.

Did You Know? The Sami language is one of the official languages of Norway.

Where to Eat:

Tromsø: Smak Restaurant offers delicious tasting menus showcasing local Arctic ingredients. Fiskekompaniet is a renowned seafood restaurant with stunning harbor views. For budget-friendly bites, head to the bustling Tromsø Public Market.

Smak Address: Stakkevollvegen 39, 9010 Tromsø, Norway.

Fiskekompaniet Address: Killengreens gate, 9008 Tromsø, Norway.

Tromsø Public Market Address: Tromsøya, 9008 Tromsø, Norway.

Alta: Restaurant Sami Siida Alta serves up delicious Sami cuisine with wonderful views.

Restaurant Sami Siida Alta Address: Øytunveien 4, 9518 Alta, Norway.

Nordkapp: Fish Restaurant Nordkapphallen serves fish burgers, soup, and dishes made with fish with panoramic views of the Arctic Ocean. The nearby Corner Spiseri is a cozy spot for drinks and comfort foods.

Fish Restaurant Nordkapp Address: Skarsvagveien 10, 9763 Skarsvag, Norway.

Corner Spiseri Address: Fiskeriveien 2A, 9750 Honnigsvag, Norway.

Shopping Guide:

Tromsø: Storgata is the main shopping street in Tromsø, lined with international brands and local boutiques. For souvenirs, visit Tromsø Gift and Souvenir Shop AS or the Polar Museum gift shop.

Storgata Address: 9008 Tromsø, Norway.

Tromsø Gift and Souvenir Shop AS Address: Strandgata 36, 9008 Tromsø, Norway.

Polar Museum Gift Shop Address: Sondre Tollbodgate 11B, 9008 Tromsø, Norway.

Alta: The Amfi Alta shopping mall has a mix of local stores and major chains.

Address: Markedsgata 21-25, 9510 Alta, Norway.

Senja: The village of Finnsnes has a few small shops and a supermarket.

Finnmark Plateau: Karasjok and Kautokeino have small stores selling Sami handicrafts and souvenirs.

Nordkapp: The Nordkapphallen gift shop has a variety of souvenirs related to the North Cape. The nearby Honningsvåg has a few small shops selling groceries and clothing.

Nordkapphallen Gift Shop Address: North Cape, E69, 9764 Nordkapp, Norway.

Hammerfest: The Sjøgata shopping street is lined with stores selling clothing, souvenirs, and local crafts. The Nissen Hammerfest Senter AS is a good option for everyday items.

The Nissen Hammerfest Senter AS Address: Sjogata 9, 9600 Hammerfest, Norway.

Entertainment:

Tromsø: The Mack Brewery offers tours and beer tastings. The Kulturhuset, or "Kultural House," hosts concerts, theater productions, and art exhibitions. For nightlife, check out Skarven Pub or Blårock for live music.

Mack Brewery Address: Musegata 1, 9008 Tromsø, Norway.

Kulturhuset Address: Erling Bandsunds plass 1, 9008 Tromsø, Norway.

Skarven Pub Address: Strandtorget 1, 9008 Tromsø, Norway.

Blårock Address: Strandgata 14, 9008 Tromsø, Norway.

Alta: The Sorrisniva Igloo Hotel offers a unique dining experience and an ice bar. The Northern Lights Cathedral hosts concerts and events throughout the year.

Sorrisniva Igloo Hotel Address: Sorrisniva 20, 9518 Alta, Norway.

Finnmark Plateau: The Sami Siida in Karasjok hosts traditional Sami storytelling and music performances. The Finnsnes Cinema shows the latest movies. The Kautokeino Sámi Center offers reindeer herding demonstrations and cultural workshops.

Sami Siida Address: Beskangeaidnu 52, 9730 Karasjok, Norway.

Finnsnes Cinema Address: Radhusveien 8, 9300 Finnsnes, Norway.

Kautokeino Sámi Center Address: Hannuluohkka 45, 9520 Kautokeino, Norway.

Nordkapp: The Nordkapphallen has a multimedia exhibition detailing the history of the North Cape. The Honningsvåg Cruise Terminal is a popular spot for live music and events.

Hammerfest: The Royal and Ancient Polar Bear Society Museum is a fun and quirky attraction. The Meridian Column offers panoramic views of the city.

The Royal and Ancient Polar Bear Society Museum Address: Strandgata 29, 9600 Hammefest, Norway.

Did You Know? The Northern Lights, or Aurora Borealis, are most visible in Troms og Finnmark from September to April.

Sports and Leisure:

Tromsø: Hiking, biking, and kayaking are popular activities in the summer months. In the winter, enjoy skiing, snowboarding, and snowmobiling on the surrounding mountains. The Tromsø Cable Car offers stunning views of the city and fjords.

Alta: Alta Canyon is an excellent spot for hiking and rock climbing. Altafjord is a popular destination for kayaking and fishing. In the winter, try cross-country skiing, snowshoeing, and dog sledding.

Finnmark Plateau: Kautokeino and Karasjok are gateways to the Arctic wilderness, offering opportunities for snowmobiling, dog sledding, and reindeer herding experiences. The Finnmarksvidda National Park is a vast expanse of tundra perfect for cross-country skiing, hiking, and wildlife watching.

Nordkapp: Hiking trails around the North Cape offer stunning views of the Arctic Ocean. In the summer, try sea kayaking and birdwatching. In the winter, witness the spectacular "midnight sun" phenomenon.

Hammerfest: The Hammerfest Ski Stadium is a popular destination for visitors who enjoy cross-country skiing and biathlon. The surrounding mountains offer alpine skiing and snowboarding opportunities. In the summer, enjoy hiking and fishing in the nearby islands.

Accommodations:

Troms og Finnmark offers a variety of accommodation options, from luxury hotels and cabins to budget-friendly hostels and campsites. Here are some highlights:

Tromsø: Thon Hotel Tromsø is a modern hotel with stunning city views. The Aurora Borealis Apartments offer a special experience with private balconies for private Northern Lights viewing. The Tromsø Camping is a great option for budget travelers.

Thon Hotel Tromsø Address: Gronnegata 50, 9008 Tromsø, Norway.

Tromsø Camping Address: Arthur Arntzens Veg 10, 9020 Tromsdalen, Norway.

Alta: Sorrisniva Igloo Hotel is a must-try for a truly unique stay in an igloo hotel. Rica Hotel Alta is a comfortable hotel with a central location.

Sorrisniva Igloo Hotel Address: Sorrisniva 20, 9518 Alta, Norway.

Rica Hotel Alta Address: Lokkeveien 61, 9509 Alta, Norway.

Senja: Senja Fjordhotell has cabins and rooms with breathtaking fjord views. Hamn i Senja offers cozy cabins in front of a fishing dock and a restaurant below. Norwegian wild has cabins and a campsite fit for glamping for a nature-oriented experience.

Senja Fjordhotell Address: Dragoyveien 28, 9392 Stonglandseidet, Norway.

Hamn i Senja Address: Hamnveien 1145, 9385 Skaland, Norway.

Norwegian Wild: Tranoyveien 2002, 9304 Vangsvik, Norway.

Finnmark Plateau: Thon Hotel Kautokeino offers comfortable rooms and has a restaurant within the hotel. Engholm Husky has wooden cabins for a truly authentic stay.

Thon Hotel Kautokeino Address: Biedjovahheluodda 2, 9520 Kautokeino, Norway.

Engholm Husky Address: Avjovargeaidnu 654, 9730 Karajok, Norway.

Nordkapp: Arctic Hotel Nordkapp is located right at the North Cape, offering stunning views and easy access to the main attractions. The Scandic Nordkapp is a good option near the North Cape and has a wonderful view of the lake.

Arctic Hotel Nordkapp Address: Storgata 12 A, 9750 Honningsvag, Norway.

Scandic Nordkapp Address: Skipsfjorden, 9762 Honningsvag, Norway.

Hammerfest: The Scandic Hammerfest is a modern hotel in a central location. The Thon Hotel Hammerfest is another comfortable option with harbor views. The Storvannet NAF Camping AS is a budget-friendly choice for campers and caravanners.

Scandic Hammerfest Address: Soroygata 15, 9600 Hammerfest, Norway.

Thon Hotel Hammerfest Address: Strandgata 2-4, 9600 Hammerfest, Norway.

Storvannet NAF Camping AS Address: Storvannsveien 103, 9603 Hammerfest, Norway.

Remember:

- Troms og Finnmark is a seasonal destination. The best time to visit for outdoor activities is from June to September, while the winter months are ideal for seeing the Northern Lights.

- Dress warmly, especially in the winter, as temperatures can drop well below freezing.

- Be prepared for unpredictable weather conditions. Pack layers and waterproof clothing.

- Respect the local culture and environment. Leave no trace and be mindful of wildlife.

With its stunning scenery, rich culture, and endless adventure opportunities, Troms og Finnmark is a destination that will leave you speechless. So, pack your bags, book your trip, and prepare to be amazed by the Arctic wonderland!

Nordland: Norway's Majestic North

A vast and breathtaking county in northern Norway, Nordland beckons with its rugged coastlines, soaring mountains, and vibrant fishing villages. From the dramatic peaks of the Lofoten Islands to the roaring rapids of Saltstraumen, Nordland offers an unparalleled blend of natural beauty, rich culture, and endless adventure. Whether you're a seasoned hiker seeking challenging trails, a kayaking enthusiast yearning for mirror-like fjords, or a family looking for unforgettable experiences under the midnight sun, Nordland has something to enthrall everyone.

Historical Background:

Nordland has been inhabited for millennia and has evidence of Viking settlements dating back to the 9th century. Fishing has always been the region's lifeblood, and the coastal culture thrives on traditions passed down through generations. In the 19th century, the discovery of vast mineral deposits brought a boom in mining and industrialization, shaping the landscape and character of some areas. Today, Nordland is a thriving modern region that balances its industrial heritage with a deep respect for its natural beauty and cultural traditions.

Main Attractions:

Lofoten Islands: This archipelago of dramatic peaks, turquoise waters, and fishing villages is a must-visit for any Nordland adventure. Hike to the iconic Reinebringen peak, kayak through the glassy waters of Nusfjord, and discover Viking history at the Lofotr Viking Museum.

As of the writing of this book, the opening hours for the Lofotr Viking Museum are every day from 10 am to 5 pm, but please always double-check the opening hours online should there have been any slight change in their schedule.

Discover Viking history at the Lofotr Viking Museum.[63]

Bodø: This vibrant city offers a mix of cultural attractions and natural wonders. Explore the Norwegian Aviation Museum, marvel at the Saltstraumen tidal current, and catch a glimpse of the Northern Lights during winter. For a hidden gem near Bodø, visit Mjelle, a village with a picturesque harbor and stunning coastal views.

As of the writing of this book, the opening hours for the Norwegian Aviation Museum are Monday to Friday from 10 am to 4 pm, and Saturday and Sunday from 11 AM to 5 PM. However, please always double-check the opening hours online should there be any slight changes in their schedule.

Norwegian Aviation Museum Address: Bortindgata 35B, 8004 Bodø, Norway.

For a hidden gem near Bodø, visit Mjelle.[64]

Saltfjellet-Svartisen National Park: This vast mountain park is a paradise for hikers of all levels. Experienced adventurers can tackle the challenging peaks of the Svartisen glacier, while families can enjoy scenic walks along the Rallarvegen, an old railway track turned hiking trail.

As of the writing of this book, the normal opening hours daily are all 24 hours of the day, but please always double-check the opening hours online should there have been any slight change in their schedule.

Saltfjellet-Svartisen National Park Address: Rana Municipality, Norway.

This vast mountain park is a paradise for hikers of all levels.[65]

Haukland and Kvalvika Beaches: These hidden gems offer pristine white sand, turquoise waters, and stunning backdrops. Relax on the beach, swim in the crystal-clear water, or hike along the dramatic cliffs.

As of the writing of this book, the normal opening hours daily are all 24 hours of the day, but please always double-check the opening hours online should there have been any slight change in their schedule.

These hidden gems offer pristine white sand, turquoise waters, and stunning backdrops.[66]

Transport:

Getting around Nordland requires careful planning because of its size and diverse terrain. The best way to explore is by car, offering flexibility and access to remote areas. However, there is a good public transport system with buses and trains connecting major towns and cities. Ferries are crucial for reaching the Lofoten Islands and other coastal areas. Consider purchasing a travel pass for discounted fares on public transportation.

Experiences:

Lofoten Islands Adventure: Hike the iconic Reinebringen trail, kayak through the fjords, join a fishing tour, or learn to surf the Arctic waves.

Northern Lights Chase: Witness the mesmerizing dance of the Aurora Borealis in the winter months, with Bodø offering a prime viewing location.

Viking History: Immerse yourself in Viking history at the Lofotr Viking Museum, explore the remains of Viking settlements, and learn about their fascinating way of life.

Saltstraumen Maelstrom: Witness the world's strongest tidal current in action, with boat tours offering a front-row seat to this natural spectacle.

Midnight Sun Hike: Hike under the midnight sun in the summer months, experiencing the unusual light and atmosphere of the Arctic summer.

Family Fun:

Lofoten Aquarium: Discover the diverse marine life of the Arctic at this interactive aquarium in Kabelvåg.

Address: Sorvanganveien 28, 8310 Kabelvag, Norway.

Saltstraumen Wildlife Watching: Spot seals, whales, and porpoises in the swirling waters of Saltstraumen.

Lofotr Viking Museum: Kids will love exploring the reconstructed Viking longhouse and learning about Viking games and traditions.

Beach Day: Build sandcastles, swim in crystal-clear water, and picnic on Haukland or Kvalvika's pristine beaches.

Bodø Cable Car: Take a scenic ride up the cable car for panoramic views of the city and surrounding mountains.

Did You Know? The world's strongest maelstrom, Saltstraumen, can reach speeds of up to 20 knots.

Where to Eat:

Lofoten: Fresh seafood is the star of the show in Lofoten. Try Brygga Restaurant and Bar in Kabelvag, which serves a variety of international cuisines and authentic Norwegian fish dishes.

Address: Torget 8310, 8310 Kabelvag, Norway.

Bodø: Enjoy a delicious meal at Roast Restaurant and Bar, known for their fiskesuppet and Cod loin. Grab a burger at Burgasm Bodø or a traditional Norwegian pølse (hot dog) from the street vendors for a casual meal.

Roast Restaurant and Bar Address: Tollbugata 5, 8006 Bodø, Norway.

Burgasm Bodø Address: Havnegata 1, 8006 Bodø, Norway.

Saltfjellet-Svartisen National Park: Cozy mountain lodges offer traditional Norwegian dishes like reindeer stew and cloudberries. Pack a picnic lunch with local cheeses and smoked meats to enjoy during your hikes.

Shopping Guide:

Lofoten: Explore the shops in Reine, Svolvær, and Henningsvær for locally made crafts, souvenirs, and outdoor gear. The Svolvær Torget market offers a variety of local products, from fresh fish to Sami handicrafts.

Bodø: Bodø Storsenter is the largest shopping center in Nordland, with a mix of international brands and local stores. For souvenirs, visit the Saltstraumen Visitor Center or the Bodø Aviation Museum gift shop.

Bodø Storsenter Address: Verkstedveien 1, 8008 Bodø, Norway.

Saltfjellet-Svartisen National Park: Souvenir shops at mountain lodges like Saltfjellet Vandrerhjem sell maps, hiking gear, and locally made crafts.

Did You Know? The Lofotr Viking Museum in Borg houses one of the world's largest and best-preserved Viking longhouses.

Entertainment:

Lofoten: Experience the vibrant nightlife scene in Svolvær or Henningsvær, with live music at bars like Styrhuset Pub. Enjoy outdoor concerts and festivals like the Arctic Film Festival in the summer.

Styrhuset Pub Address: Fiskergata 8300, 8300 Svolvær, Norway.

Bodø: Enjoy live music at one of Bodø's many cafes and bars. The Bodø Spektrum arena hosts concerts, sporting events, and other entertainment throughout the year.

Bodø Spektrum Address: Plassmyrveien 11, 8008 Bodø, Norway.

Saltfjellet-Svartisen National Park: Relax by the fireplace in the cozy common rooms of mountain lodges and enjoy board games or stargazing under the Arctic sky.

Hidden Gems: Haukland Beach offers stunning sunsets and opportunities for bonfire gatherings. In Mjelle, enjoy a boat trip on the scenic Saltstraumen maelstrom.

Sports and Leisure:

Lofoten: Hiking, kayaking, fishing, and surfing are popular activities in Lofoten. Explore the dramatic mountains, paddle through calm fjords, cast your line for Arctic cod, or ride the waves at Unstad Beach. In the winter, enjoy skiing, snowboarding, and snowmobiling.

Bodø: Bodø is a haven for outdoor enthusiasts. Hike to the top of Keipen mountain for stunning views, kayak in Saltstraumen, or try your hand at rock climbing on the dramatic cliffs. In the winter, go skiing or snowboarding at the Bodø Alpine Center.

Saltfjellet-Svartisen National Park: Hike on the numerous trails in the park, from challenging glacier climbs to family-friendly walks along the Rallarveien. Fish in the mountain lakes, try white-water rafting on the Sulis River or enjoy cross-country skiing in the winter.

Hidden Gems: Haukland Beach and Kvalvika Beach offer excellent surfing conditions for experienced surfers. In Mjelle, go for a relaxing bike ride along the scenic coastal road or explore the nearby islands by kayak.

Accommodations:

Lofoten: Choose from a variety of accommodations in Lofoten, from traditional Rorbu cabins perched on stilts to cozy guesthouses and modern hotels. For a unique experience, try glamping in a yurt or camping under the midnight sun.

Bodø: Choose from city-center accommodations near the harbor or a quieter stay at a hotel on the outskirts of town with stunning mountain views. For families, the Scandic Havet Hotel has an indoor pool and playground.

Scandic Havet Hotel Address: Tollbugata 5, 8006 Bodø, Norway.

Saltfjellet-Svartisen National Park: Experience the rustic charm of mountain lodges like Saltfjellet Hotel Arctic Circle. These lodges have comfortable rooms, hearty meals, and stunning views of the surrounding mountains. For a more adventurous option, try camping in designated areas within the park.

Hidden Gems: For a truly unique stay near Haukland Beach, consider the Skreda Rorbusuiter, where you can rent traditional Rorbu cabins with modern amenities. In Mjelle, the Kjerringgoy Bryggehotell offers comfortable rooms and a friendly atmosphere in a village setting.

Planning Your Nordland Adventure:

Nordland's vastness and diverse terrain require careful planning. Here are some tips to make your adventure smooth and unforgettable:

- **Decide When to Visit:** Summer offers long days, midnight sun, and ideal conditions for hiking, kayaking, and other outdoor activities. Winter brings the Northern Lights, skiing opportunities, and a magical winter wonderland atmosphere. Spring and autumn offer milder temperatures and fewer crowds.

- **Choose Your Transportation:** Renting a car offers the most flexibility, especially if you plan to explore remote areas. Public transportation, including buses and trains, connects major towns and cities, while ferries are essential for reaching the Lofoten Islands and other coastal areas.

- **Pack for All Weather Conditions:** Nordland's weather can be unpredictable, so pack layers for all temperatures, waterproof gear for rain and snow, and comfortable hiking shoes.

- **Respect the Environment:** Leave no trace, dispose of waste responsibly, and be mindful of wildlife and local traditions.

- **Embrace the Adventure:** Nordland offers endless opportunities for exploration and discovery. Be spontaneous, embrace the unexpected, and create memories that will last a lifetime.

With its breathtaking scenery, rich culture, and endless adventure, Nordland is waiting to be explored. And so, your journey through Norway's enchanting landscapes concludes in the Arctic North. You've climbed snow-capped peaks, sailed through crystalline fjords, wandered villages, and tasted the soul of this remarkable nation. May these stories and experiences linger in your memory, inviting you to return and write your chapters in the ever-evolving saga of Norway. Bon voyage, and remember, the magic of Norway always awaits, beckoning you to unveil its hidden wonders.

Chapter 9: Itineraries and Programs

Norway, the land of fjords, villages, and rugged coastlines, offers a smorgasbord of experiences for every kind of traveler. Whether you're seeking adrenaline-pumping adventures, tranquil fjord cruises, or vibrant city escapes, Norway has something for you. This chapter guides you through diverse itineraries tailored to specific themes or traveler types, allowing you to curate your perfect Nordic adventure.

An adventure awaits; mark your calendar.[67]

Winter Wonderland (1 Week)

Theme: Embrace the magic of winter in Norway, including skiing and snowshoeing to experiencing the Northern Lights.

Target Traveler: Winter sports enthusiasts, couples seeking a romantic getaway.

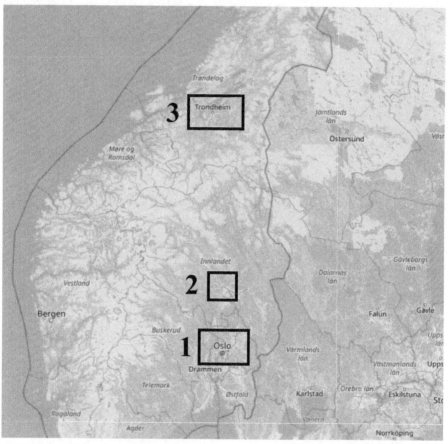

Full Winter Wonderland trip, starting at Osolo (1) then Lillehammer (2) then Trondheim (3) before returning to Oslo.[68]

Day 1: Oslo

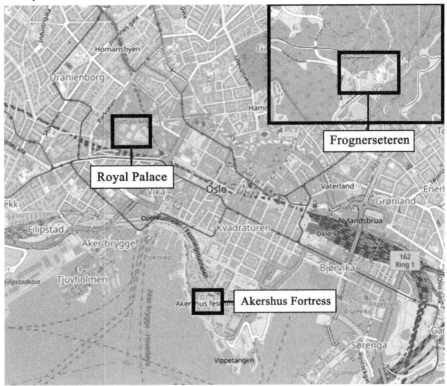

Day 1.[69]

Morning: Start with a snowy city walk, visiting the Royal Palace and Akershus Fortress.

Royal Palace QR Code.

Akershus Fortress QR Code.

Afternoon: Walk about 1 km to Oslo Central train station then take Line 1 to Frognerseteren. Learn to cross-country ski at Frognerseteren, surrounded by snow-covered forests.

Frognersteren QR Code.

Evening: Enjoy a winter wonderland dinner at a cozy restaurant overlooking the snow-dusted Oslo skyline.

Day 2: Oslo to Lillehammer

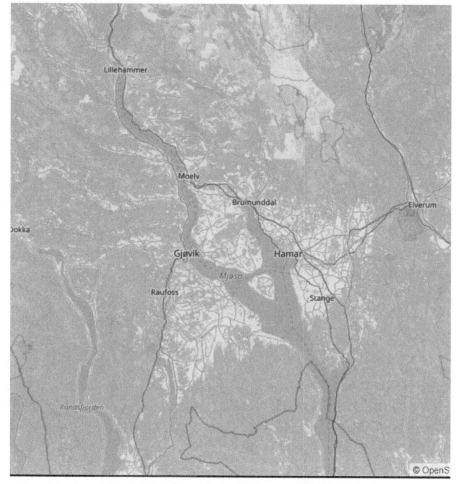

Lillehammer (north-west) and Lake Mjøsa[70]

Morning: Take the train to Lillehammer (2 hours), the host city of the 1994 Winter Olympics. Visit the Olympic ski jumps and museums.

Afternoon: Go ice skating on Lake Mjøsa at the Vingnesvika ice skating track.

Evening: Warm up in a traditional Norwegian cabin with a crackling fireplace and hearty winter stew.

Day 3: Lillehammer and Sleigh Ride

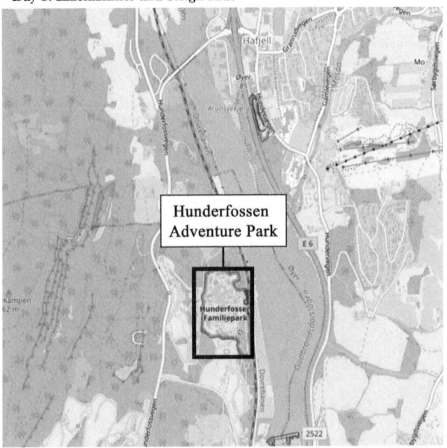

Day 3.[71]

Morning: Embark on a magical sleigh ride through the snowy forests of Lillehammer, surrounded by pristine landscapes.

Afternoon: Visit the Hunderfossen Adventure Park, home to ice sculptures, snow activities, and thrilling rides.

Huderfossen Adventure Park QR Code.

Evening: Indulge in a traditional Norwegian dinner, savoring local delicacies and festive cheer.

Day 4: Trondheim and the Northern Lights

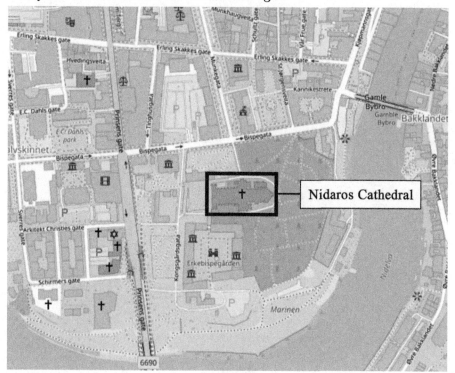

Day 4.[72]

Morning: Take the scenic train journey to Trondheim (4 to 5 hours), the city known for its colorful wooden houses and Nidaros Cathedral.

Nidaros Cathedral QR Code.

Afternoon: Explore the city's museums and vibrant Christmas markets, filled with twinkling lights and festive aromas.

Evening: Join a guided Northern Lights tour, venturing away from the city lights to witness the Aurora Borealis dance across the winter sky.

Day 5: Trondheim and Coastal Exploration

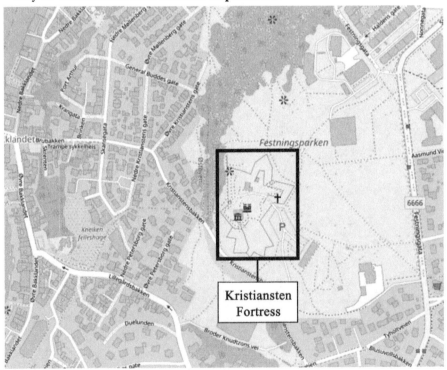

Day 5.[73]

Morning: Visit the Kristiansten Fortress, offering panoramic views of Trondheim and the surrounding fjords.

Kristiansten Fortress QR Code.

Afternoon: Embark on a coastal fjord cruise, admiring the snow-capped mountains and frozen landscapes from the water.

Evening: Sample traditional Norwegian fish dishes at a cozy harborside restaurant.

Day 6: Trondheim to Oslo

Morning: Enjoy a leisurely breakfast and last-minute shopping in Trondheim's boutiques.

Afternoon: Take the train back to Oslo (7 hours), reflecting on the unforgettable winter experiences.

Evening: Have a final farewell dinner in Oslo, celebrating the memories of your Norwegian winter adventure.

Day 7: Departure

Morning: Enjoy a final stroll through Oslo's streets, taking last-minute photos and savoring the city's ambiance.

Afternoon: Depart from Oslo with a heart full of winter magic and unforgettable Norwegian experiences.

Coastal Charm and Island Hopping (1 Week)

Theme: Explore the beauty of Norway's stunning coastline, island communities, and hidden coves.

Target Traveler: Nature lovers, beach enthusiasts, and those seeking relaxation and scenic beauty.

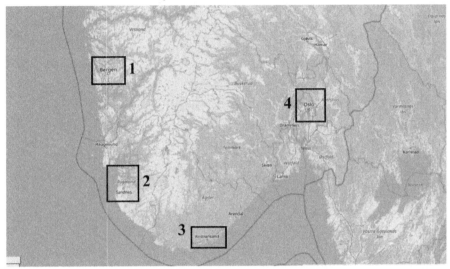

Full trip, starting at Bergen (1) followed by Stavanger (2), then Kristiansand (3) before finally ending at Oslo (4)[74]

Day 1: Bergen

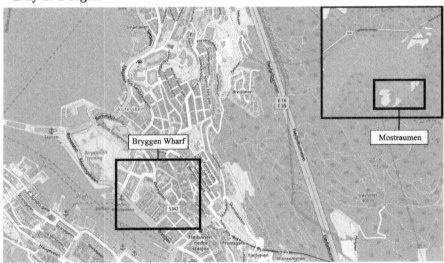

Day 1.[75]

Morning: Start your journey in Bergen, the "City of Seven Hills," and wander through the vibrant Bryggen Wharf, lined with colorful wooden houses and bustling fish markets.

Bryggen Wharf QR Code.

Afternoon: Take a 4-hour roundtrip fjord cruise to Mostraumen. Admire views of the mountainsides, waterfalls, and the Mostraumen strait.

Mostraumen QR Code.

Evening: Return to Bergen and savor a delicious seafood dinner at a harborside restaurant, soaking in the city's lively atmosphere.

Day 2: Bergen to Stavanger

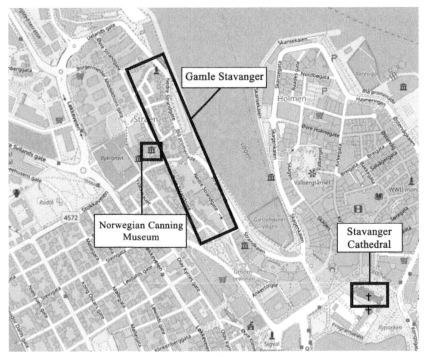

Day 2.[76]

Morning: Take a scenic coastal cruise from Bergen to Stavanger (5 to 6 hours), admiring the rugged coastline, cascading waterfalls, and fishing villages along the way.

Afternoon: Explore Stavanger's historic Gamle Stavanger neighborhood, a maze of colorful wooden houses and cobblestone streets. Walk about 80 m to learn about the region's fishing industry and historical significance at the Norwegian Canning Museum. Walk 600 m to visit the Stavanger Cathedral, one of the oldest cathedrals in Norway. Sample fresh seafood at a local restaurant, savoring the flavors of the coast.

Gamle Stavanger QR Code.

Stavanger Cathedral QR Code.

Norwegian Canning Museum QR Code.

Evening: Take a stroll along Stavanger's harborfront, enjoying the vibrant atmosphere and stunning sunset views.

Day 3: Stavanger and Island Hopping

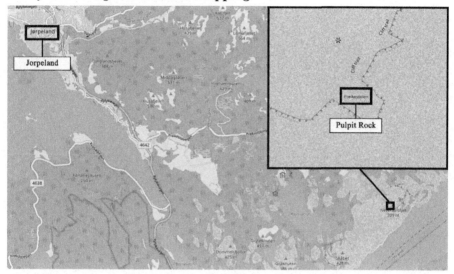

Day 3.[77]

Morning: Rent a kayak or join a guided tour to explore the islands near Stavanger, discovering hidden coves and deserted beaches. Spot harbor seals basking on the rocks and enjoy the tranquility of the pristine coastline.

Afternoon and Evening: Take a boat trip to the Lysefjord (3-4 hours), known for its Pulpit Rock, a towering cliff offering breathtaking views of the fjord. Enjoy a picnic dinner on the shore, surrounded by the majestic scenery.

Pulpit Rock QR Code.

Day 4: Stavanger to Kristiansand

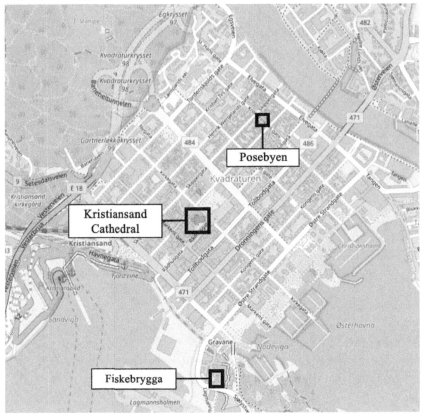

Day 4.[78]

Morning: Take the train from Stavanger to Kristiansand (3 to 4 hours), passing through idyllic farmland, villages, and dramatic coastal landscapes.

Afternoon: Explore Kristiansand's bustling harbor and old town. Visit the Kristiansand Cathedral and the Posebyen, a vibrant district filled with colorful houses and art galleries.

Kristiansand Cathedral QR Code.

Posebyen QR Code.

Evening: Enjoy a delicious dinner at Fiskebrygga, Kristiansand's fish market, sampling fresh seafood and local delicacies.

Fiskebrygga QR Code.

Day 5: Kristiansand and the Southern Coast

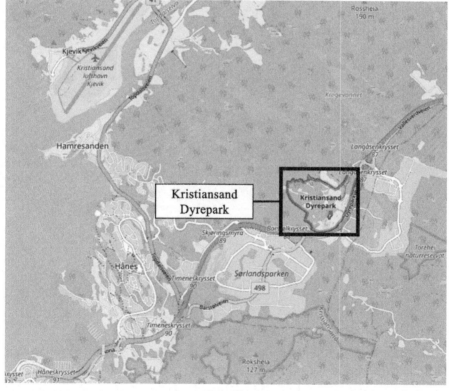

Day 5.[79]

Morning: Rent a bike and cycle the scenic bike paths along Kristiansand's coastline, stopping at sandy beaches and seaside towns. Take a dip in the refreshing waters or build sandcastles on the beach.

Afternoon: Visit the Kristiansand Dyrepark, home to Scandinavian animals and exciting rides, perfect for a fun family outing.

Kristiansand Dyrepark QR Code.

Evening: Enjoy a relaxing evening at one of Kristiansand's many beaches, watching the sunset paint the sky in vibrant colors.

Day 6: Kristiansand to Oslo

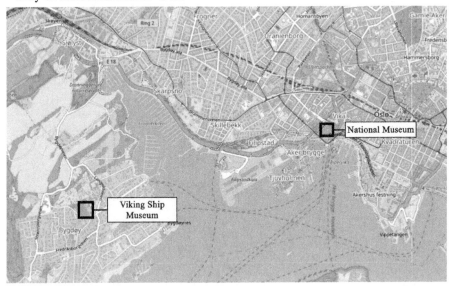

Day 6.[80]

Morning: Take the train back to Oslo (5 hours), enjoying the scenic journey through the Norwegian countryside.

Afternoon: Spend the afternoon exploring Oslo's museums and cultural attractions, such as the Viking Ship Museum or the National Museum.

Viking Ship Musuem QR Code.

National Gallery QR Code.

Evening: Have a farewell dinner in Oslo, celebrating the memories of your coastal adventure and island-hopping experience.

Day 7: Departure

Morning: Enjoy a final stroll through Oslo's streets, soaking in the city's atmosphere and saying goodbye to Norway.

Afternoon: Take your flight home, carrying with you the memories of Norway's coastline, hidden coves, and the endless beauty of its islands.

Northern Lights Chase and Arctic Adventure (1 Week)

Theme: Embark on a thrilling adventure through the Arctic Circle, chasing the mesmerizing Northern Lights and experiencing the unique beauty of the far north.

Target Traveler: Adventure seekers, photographers, and those seeking unique, off-the-beaten-path experiences.

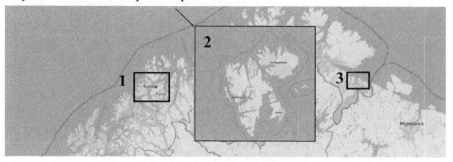

Full trip, starting at Tromso, then Svalbard islands and ending at Kirkenes[81]

Day 1: Tromsø

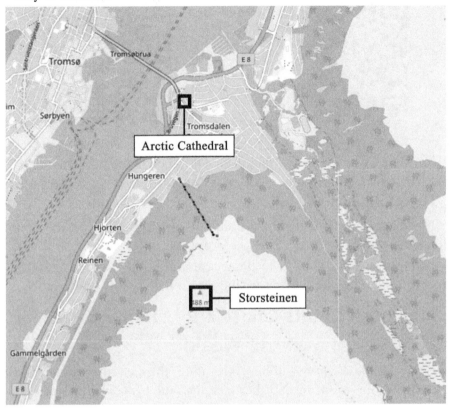

Day 1.[82]

Morning: Arrive in Tromsø, the vibrant "Gateway to the Arctic." Explore the city's colorful waterfront and visit the iconic Arctic Cathedral, a masterpiece of modern architecture.

Arctic Cathedral QR Code.

Afternoon: Take a funicular ride up Storsteinen, enjoying breathtaking panoramic views of Tromsø and the surrounding fjords.

Storsteinen QR Code.

Evening: Join a guided Northern Lights tour, venturing away from the city lights to witness the awe-inspiring Aurora Borealis dance across the Arctic sky. Capture stunning photographs of this natural light show.

Day 2: Tromsø and Sami Culture

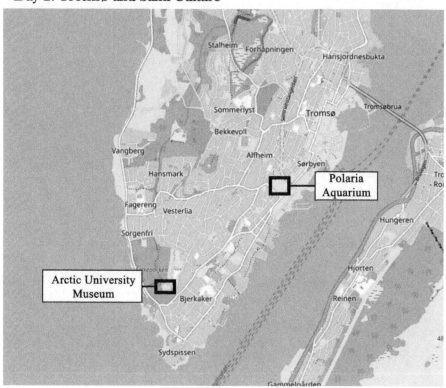

Day 2.[83]

Morning: Learn about the indigenous Sami culture at the Arctic University Museum, where you can see traditional clothing, artifacts, and exhibits on Sami history and way of life.

Arctic University Museum QR Code.

Afternoon: Visit the Polaria Aquarium, home to Arctic marine life like polar bears, seals, and walruses. Learn about the importance of conservation in the Arctic region.

To get to Polaria Aquarium, walk 350 m to the Folkeparken Bus Stop then take Bus 34 to Polaria. The Polaria Aquarium is a 140 m walk from the bus stop.

Polaria Aquarium QR Code.

Evening: Enjoy a traditional Sami dinner at a cozy restaurant, savoring reindeer stew, cloudberries, and other local delicacies. Listen to traditional Sami music and stories around a crackling fireplace.

Day 3: Tromsø to Svalbard

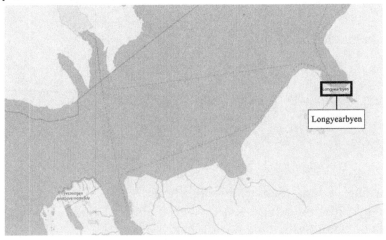

Day 3.[84]

Morning: Take a flight to Longyearbyen (almost 2 hours), the capital of Svalbard, an archipelago midway between Norway and the North Pole. Immerse yourself in the Arctic wilderness and the unique atmosphere of this remote settlement.

Afternoon: Embark on a snowmobile or dogsled adventure through the breathtaking Svalbard landscape, spotting Arctic wildlife like polar bears, reindeer, and arctic foxes.

Evening: Enjoy a delicious dinner at a local restaurant, savoring fresh seafood and traditional Svalbard dishes. Relax and soak up the midnight sun, visible in Svalbard during summer.

Day 4: Svalbard and Ice Caves

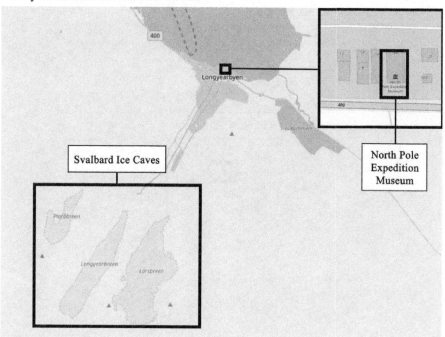

Day 4.[85]

Morning: Explore the otherworldly beauty of the Svalbard Ice Caves, natural tunnels formed within glaciers. Marvel at the ice formations and the fascinating play of light and colors.

Afternoon: Visit the North Pole Expedition Museum and learn about Arctic exploration and the history of Svalbard. See artifacts from polar expeditions and discover the challenges of living in this extreme environment.

North Pole Expedition Museum QR Code.

Evening: Enjoy a traditional "Polar BBQ" under the open sky, grilling fresh meat and vegetables under the mesmerizing Aurora Borealis.

Day 5: Svalbard to Kirkenes

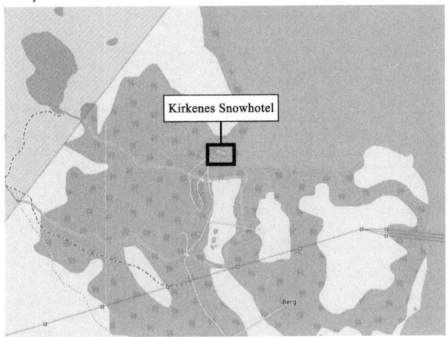

Day 5.[86]

Morning: Take a flight to Kirkenes (almost 4 hours), a town on the border with Russia, known for its unique location and proximity to the Barents Sea.

Afternoon: Visit the Kirkenes Snowhotel, built entirely of snow and ice, and experience the magic of sleeping in a sub-zero environment.

Kirkenes Snowhotel QR Code.

Evening: Join a King Crab Safari, venturing onto the Barents Sea to catch and savor these giant crabs, a local delicacy. Learn about sustainable fishing practices in the Arctic region.

Day 6: Kirkenes and Snowmobile Adventure

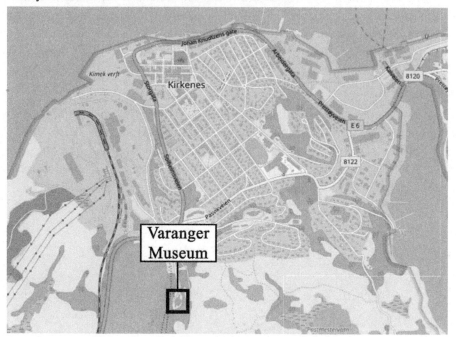

Day 6.s[87]

Morning: Embark on a thrilling snowmobile adventure through the frozen landscapes near Kirkenes, crossing the border into Russia for a truly unique experience.

Afternoon: Visit Varanger Museum and explore the multicultural history of Northern Norway. Enjoy lunch at a nearby restaurant.

Varanger Museum QR Code.

Evening: Enjoy a farewell dinner at a local restaurant in Kirkenes, reflecting on your unforgettable Arctic adventure.

Day 7: Departure

Morning: Take your flight home from Kirkenes, carrying the memories of the mesmerizing Northern Lights, the Arctic wilderness, and the unique cultures you encountered with you.

Afternoon: Arrive home, forever changed by your Arctic adventure, with stories to share and a newfound appreciation for the beauty and fragility of the far north.

These are just a few examples of the many exciting itineraries you can create when exploring Norway. With its diverse landscapes, rich culture, and endless outdoor activities, Norway has something to offer everyone. So, pack your bags, choose your adventure, and get ready to experience the magic of Norway!

Bonus Chapter: Useful Norwegian Survival Phrases

Embarking on your Norwegian adventure with a few key phrases tucked away in your pocket will enhance your experience and open doors to deeper cultural immersion and richer interactions with local people. Mastering basic communication goes beyond getting from point A to point B. It paves the way for genuine connections and authentic memories.

Essential Greetings and Farewells

- **Hello:** Hei (hey) – Pronounced "hay" like the English word.
- **Good Morning:** God morgen (gow mor-gen) – Pronounced "gow" like in "cow" and "mor-gen" like "mor" in "morning."
- **Good Evening:** God kveld (gow kvelt) – Pronounced "gow" like in "cow" and "kvelt" like "belt" without the "b."
- **Goodbye:** Ha det (hah deh) – Pronounced "hah" like in "happy" and "deh" like the first syllable in "debt."

Navigating Daily Situations

- **Please:** Vær så snill (vair saw shill) – Pronounced "vair" like the first syllable in "very," "saw" like "sawdust," and "shill" like "chill" without the "ch."
- **Thank You:** Takk (tahk) – Pronounced like "tuck" in "tuck my shirt in."

- **Thank You Very Much:** Takk skal du ha (tahk shall doo hah) –
Pronounced "tahk" like in "tuck," "shall" like in "shallow," "doo"
like the "oo" in "boot," and "hah" like the last syllable in "haha."

- **Excuse Me/Sorry:** Unnskyld (oon-sheeld) – Pronounced "oon"
like the first syllable in "under," "shee" like in "she," and "ld"
like the "l" in "milk."

- **Do You Speak English?:** Snakker du engelsk? (snak-ker doo
engelska?) – Pronounced "snak-ker" like "snac" with a rolled "r,"
"doo" like "oo" in "boot," "engelska" like "in-gel-ska" with a hard
"g."

Essential Needs and Emergencies

- **I Need Help:** Jeg trenger hjelp (yeh tren-ger yelp) – Pronounced
"yeh" like the "y" in "yellow," "tren-ger" like "tren" in "trenches"
with a rolled "r," and "yelp" like the word "yelp."

- **Where Is...?** Hvor er...? (vor air...?) – Pronounced "vor" like
"war," and "air" like the first syllable in "airport."

- **I Don't Understand:** Jeg forstår ikke (yeh for-står eek-keh) –
Pronounced "yeh" like the "y" in "yellow," "for-står" like "four"
with a rolled "r" and a hard "å," and "eek-keh" like "ick" with a
hard "k."

- **Can You Speak Slower?** Kan du snakke saktere? (kan doo snak-
keh sak-teh-reh?) – Pronounced "kan" like "can," "doo" like
"oo" in "boot," "snak-keh" like "snac" with a rolled "r," and "sak-
teh-reh" like "sac-ter" with a rolled "r" and a hard "e."

- **I'm Allergic to...:** Jeg er allergisk mot... (yeh air ah-ler-gisk
moot...) – Pronounced "yeh" like the "y" in "yellow," "air" like
the first syllable in "airport," "ah-ler-gisk" like "allergic" with a
hard "g," "moot" like "mute."

- **Call the Police:** Ring politiet (ring po-lee-tee-eh) – Pronounced
"ring" like in "ring a bell," "po-lee-tee" like "po-lice" with a rolled
"r."

Shopping and Dining

- **How Much Is This?** Hvor mye koster dette? (vor mee kohs-ter
deht-teh?) – Pronounced "vor" like "war," "mee" like "me,"

"koahs-ter" like "cost" with a hard "å," and "deht-teh" like "det" in "det means."

- **Can I Have the Bill, Please?:** Regningen, takk. (reg-ningen, tahk) – Pronounced "reg-ningen" like "reg-nin" with a rolled "r" and a hard "g," "tahk" like in "tuck."

- **This Is Delicious!:** Dette er nydelig! (deht-teh air ny-deh-lig) – Pronounced "deht-the" like "det" in "det means," "air" like the first syllable in "airport," "ny-deh-lig" like "ny" in "new" with a hard "y" and "deh-lig" like "lig" in "ligament."

- **Do You Have Vegetarian Options?:** Har du vegetariske alternativer? (har doo veh-geh-tah-ris-keh all-ter-nah-tee-ver) – Pronounced "har" like the first syllable in "harmony," "doo" like "oo" in "boot," "veh-geh-tah-ris-keh" like "veggie-tar-ish" with a hard "g," "all-ter-nah-tee-ver" like "al-ter-na-tives" with a hard "v."

Pronunciation Tips

- Norwegian uses rolled "r"s, especially in the beginning and middle of words. Practice vibrating your tongue against the roof of your mouth to achieve the sound.

- The diphthong "ei" sounds like "ay" in "say." Examples: hei (hello), leit (sorry).

- The letter "ø" sounds like the "u" in "burn." Examples: kjøpe (buy), søt (sweet).

- The letter "æ" sounds like the "a" in "cat." Examples: æble (apple), lækker (delicious).

- Don't be afraid to make mistakes. Norwegians appreciate the effort to speak their language and are generally friendly and helpful.

Remember, even a few basic phrases can go a long way in enriching your Norwegian experience. So, don't hesitate to greet a local with a friendly "Hei!" and thank them with a heartfelt "Takk." Navigate your way through this stunning country with a smile and a sprinkle of Norwegian.

Appendix

This appendix provides a comprehensive alphabetical listing of major attractions, monuments, and museums in Norway, along with their corresponding cities or regions.

A:

- **Akershus Fortress (Oslo):** A medieval castle with panoramic city views and Viking Ship Museum.
- **Aker Brygge (Oslo):** Bustling waterfront district with restaurants, shops, and harbor cruises.
- **Alta Museum (Alta):** The museum showcases Sami culture and history, featuring outdoor rock carvings.
- **Arctic Cathedral (Tromsø):** Modern architectural masterpiece with stunning stained-glass windows.

B:

- **Bergen Fish Market (Bergen):** Vibrant market selling fresh seafood and local delicacies.
- **Bryggen Wharf (Bergen):** UNESCO-listed waterfront with colorful wooden houses and cobbled streets.

C:

- **Kristiansten Fortress (Trondheim):** This 17th-century fortress offers panoramic views of Trondheim and the surrounding fjords.

D:

- **Dyrepark Zoo (Kristiansand):** Scandinavia's largest zoo, home to animals from around the world.

F:

- **Flåm Railway (Flåm):** Scenic train journey through breathtaking mountain landscapes.
- **Fram Museum (Oslo):** Museum showcasing polar exploration, including the famed Fram ship.

G:

- **Geirangerfjord (Geiranger):** UNESCO-listed fjord known for its dramatic waterfalls and towering cliffs.
- **Gudbrandsdalen (Oppland):** Picturesque valley with traditional farms, stave churches, and hiking trails.

H:

- **Hunderfossen Winter Park (Lillehammer):** Winter wonderland with ice skating, snow activities, and thrilling rides.

J:

- **Jærbanen Train Journey (Stavanger to Kristiansand):** Scenic coastal train ride through villages and dramatic landscapes.

K:

- **Kirkenes Snowhotel (Kirkenes):** This unique hotel is built entirely of snow and ice, offering an Arctic adventure.
- **Kristiansten Fortress (Bergen):** This 17th-century fortress has panoramic views of Bergen and the surrounding mountains.

L:

- **Lofoten Islands (Northern Norway):** The Archipelago is known for its dramatic scenery, fishing villages, and midnight sun.
- **Lysefjord (Stavanger):** Scenic fjord with the iconic Pulpit Rock, a towering cliff offering breathtaking views.

M:

- **Moldefjorden (Molde):** Picturesque fjord is known for its archipelago of small islands and the Romsdalen mountains.
- **Mosjoen Island (Bergen):** Scenic island near Bergen with hiking trails, beaches, and hidden coves.

N:

- **Nidaros Cathedral (Trondheim):** Norway's largest and oldest cathedral, dating back to the 12th century.
- **North Pole Museum (Svalbard):** Museum showcasing Arctic exploration history and the challenges of living in the far north.

O:

- **Old Stavanger (Stavanger):** historic district with colorful wooden houses and cobblestone streets.
- **Oslo National Gallery (Oslo):** Renowned museum showcasing Norwegian and international art, including works by Edvard Munch.

P:

- **Polaria Aquarium (Tromsø):** Aquarium showcasing Arctic marine life, including polar bears, seals, and walruses.
- **Pulpit Rock (Stavanger):** Iconic cliff offering breathtaking views of the Lysefjord.

R:

- **Romsdalen Mountains (Molde):** Dramatic mountain range with glaciers, waterfalls, and challenging hiking trails.
- **Royal Palace (Oslo):** Official residence of the Norwegian monarch, open for public tours in the summer.

S:

- **Sami Siida (Kirkenes):** Traditional Sami village offering Einblicke into their reindeer herding culture and way of life.
- **Svalbard Ice Caves (Svalbard):** Natural tunnels within glaciers, offering a glimpse into the Arctic ice world.

T:

- **Tromsø Museum (Tromsø):** Museum showcasing Sami culture, Arctic history, and natural history exhibits.

V:

- **Viking Ship Museum (Oslo):** Renowned museum showcasing Viking ships, artifacts, and burial mounds.

X:

- **Xylophone (Bergen):** Traditional wooden instrument played in Bergen's Bryggen Wharf.

Here's another book by Captivating Travels that you might like

Welcome Aboard, Discover Your Limited-Time Free Bonus!

Hello, traveler! Welcome to the Captivating Travels family, and thanks for grabbing a copy of this book! Since you've chosen to join us on this journey, we'd like to offer you something special.

Check out the link below for a FREE Ultimate Travel Checklist eBook & Printable PDF to make your travel planning stress-free and enjoyable.

But that's not all - you'll also gain access to our exclusive email list with even more free e-books and insider travel tips. Well, what are you waiting for? Click the link below to join and embark on your next adventure with ease.

Access your bonus here:
https://livetolearn.lpages.co/checklist/
Or, Scan the QR code!

References

21 Best Places to Visit in Norway. (n.d.). Digit. https://www.godigit.com/international-travel-insurance/tourist-places/places-to-visit-in-norway

Anand, R. (2021, December 7). Top 10 Places To Visit in Norway For The Love Of History, Nature, And Architecture. Travel Triangle. https://traveltriangle.com/blog/places-to-visit-in-norway/

Austin, C. (2023, December 19). 18 Top Attractions & Things to Do in Norway. Touropia. https://www.touropia.com/tourist-attractions-in-norway/

Dearsley, B. (2022, May 26). 15 Top-Rated Tourist Attractions in Norway. Planetware. https://www.planetware.com/tourist-attractions/norway-n.htm

Places to Visit in Norway. (n.d.). Thrillophilia.com. https://www.thrillophilia.com/destinations/norway/places-to-visit

Steffensen, L. O. (2018, December 6). 20 Unmissable Attractions In Norway. Culture Trip. https://theculturetrip.com/europe/norway/articles/20-unmissable-attractions-in-norway

Things to Do in Norway. (n.d.-a). Visit Norway. https://www.visitnorway.com/things-to-do/

Things to Do in Norway. (n.d.-b). Viator. https://www.viator.com/Norway/d61

Things to Do in Oslo. (n.d.). Viator. https://www.viator.com/en-IN/Oslo/d902

Top 10 Destinations in Norway. (2016). Visit Norway. https://www.visitnorway.com/places-to-go/top-10-places-in-norway/

Image Sources

[1] *Accipite7, CC BY-SA 4.0 <https://creativecommons.org/licenses/by-sa/4.0>, via Wikimedia Commons: https://commons.wikimedia.org/wiki/File:Norway_5_unofficial_regions_map.png*

[2] *Júlio Reis and João David Tereso, CC BY-SA 2.5 <https://creativecommons.org/licenses/by-sa/2.5>, via Wikimedia Commons: https://commons.wikimedia.org/wiki/File:Norway_counties.svg*

[3] *Robert Jenssen, CC BY 3.0 <https://creativecommons.org/licenses/by/3.0>, via Wikimedia Commons: https://commons.wikimedia.org/wiki/File:Norwegian_Mountain_View_(222087405).jpeg*

[4] *Avinor Oslo lufthavn/Espen Solli, CC BY 3.0 <https://creativecommons.org/licenses/by/3.0>, via Wikimedia Commons: https://commons.wikimedia.org/wiki/File:Oslo_Airport_terminal_night_view.jpg*

[5] *Avinor Oslo lufthavn/Espen Solli, CC BY 3.0 <https://creativecommons.org/licenses/by/3.0>, via Wikimedia Commons: https://commons.wikimedia.org/wiki/File:Oslo_airport_departure_gates.jpg*

[6] *Dr. Blofeld, CC BY-SA 2.0 <https://creativecommons.org/licenses/by-sa/2.0>, via Wikimedia Commons. https://commons.wikimedia.org/wiki/File:Location_map_Norway_Oslo.png*

[7] *Geir Hval (www.MacWhale.eu), CC BY-SA 4.0 <https://creativecommons.org/licenses/by-sa/4.0>, via Wikimedia Commons: https://commons.wikimedia.org/wiki/File:Aker_Brygge_Akershus_Festning_Pipervika_Oslo_Norway_(2021.03.17).jpg*

[8] *Max Froumentin, CC BY 2.0 <https://creativecommons.org/licenses/by/2.0>, via Wikimedia Commons: https://commons.wikimedia.org/wiki/File:Ski_Jump_at_Holmenkollen.jpg*

[9] *randreu, CC BY 3.0 <https://creativecommons.org/licenses/by/3.0>, via Wikimedia Commons: https://commons.wikimedia.org/wiki/File:Norway_-_Oslo,_The_National_Museum_of_Art_-_panoramio_(3).jpg*

[10] *Andrew Shiva / Wikipedia: https://commons.wikimedia.org/wiki/File:NOR-2016-Frogner_Park-Vigeland_Installation-View_from_the_monolith.jpg*

[11] *Tore Storm Halvorsen, CC BY-SA 4.0 <https://creativecommons.org/licenses/by-sa/4.0>, via Wikimedia Commons: https://commons.wikimedia.org/wiki/File:Fram_Museum_building,_February_2018.jpg*

[12] *TUBS, CC BY-SA 3.0 <https://creativecommons.org/licenses/by-sa/3.0>, via Wikimedia Commons. https://commons.wikimedia.org/wiki/File:Ostlandet_in_Norway.svg*

[13] *Wolfmann, CC BY-SA 4.0 <https://creativecommons.org/licenses/by-sa/4.0>, via Wikimedia Commons: https://commons.wikimedia.org/wiki/File:Haugar_Vestfold_Kunstmuseum_Sj%C3%B8mannsskolen_architects_Andreas_Bjercke_Georg_Eliassen_1921_art_museum_T%C3%B8nsberg_Norway_01_2017-09-17.jpg*

[14] *Øyvind Berg, CC BY-SA 4.0 <https://creativecommons.org/licenses/by-sa/4.0>, via Wikimedia Commons: https://commons.wikimedia.org/wiki/File:Telemarkskanalen_minutt_for_minutt_-_Victoria_mellom_Kviteseidbrui_og_Sundebrui.jpg*

[15] *I, Besse, CC BY-SA 3.0 <http://creativecommons.org/licenses/by-sa/3.0/>, via Wikimedia Commons: https://commons.wikimedia.org/wiki/File:Rjukan_kirke_TRS_070603_060.jpg*

[16] *Micha L. Rieser, Attribution, via Wikimedia Commons: https://commons.wikimedia.org/wiki/File:Stavechurch-heddal.jpg*

[17] *Peulle, CC BY-SA 4.0 <https://creativecommons.org/licenses/by-sa/4.0>, via Wikimedia Commons: https://commons.wikimedia.org/wiki/File:Norsk_bergverksmuseum.jpg*

[18] *Wilhelm Joys Andersen from Oslo, Norway, CC BY-SA 2.0 <https://creativecommons.org/licenses/by-sa/2.0>, via Wikimedia Commons: https://commons.wikimedia.org/wiki/File:Hoved%C3%B8ya_aerial.jpg*

[19] *Peulle, CC BY-SA 4.0 <https://creativecommons.org/licenses/by-sa/4.0>, via Wikimedia Commons: https://commons.wikimedia.org/wiki/File:Drammen_flom_februar_2020_(21).jpg*

[20] *https://commons.wikimedia.org/wiki/File:View_of_the_Fredrikstad_bridge_from_the_fortress.jpg*

[21] *Lillehammer 2016 Youth Olympic Games from Norway, CC BY 2.0 <https://creativecommons.org/licenses/by/2.0>, via Wikimedia Commons: https://commons.wikimedia.org/wiki/File:Lysg%C3%A5rdsbakkene_Ski_jumping_Arena.jpg*

[22] *Holger Uwe Schmitt, CC BY-SA 4.0 <https://creativecommons.org/licenses/by-sa/4.0>, via Wikimedia Commons: https://commons.wikimedia.org/wiki/File:%22Das_Freilichtmuseum_Maihaugen_ist_eines_der_gr%C3%B6%C3%9Ften_Museen_Norwegens%22._(Die_Stabkirche)_01.jpg*

[23] *Annabel, CC BY-SA 3.0 <https://creativecommons.org/licenses/by-sa/3.0>, via Wikimedia Commons: https://commons.wikimedia.org/wiki/File:Jotunheimen_mountains_near_Memurubu.jpg*

[24] *Jadize44, CC BY-SA 4.0 <https://creativecommons.org/licenses/by-sa/4.0>, via Wikimedia Commons: https://commons.wikimedia.org/wiki/File:Rondane_National_Park._Norway._04.jpg*

[25] *kallerna, CC BY-SA 4.0 <https://creativecommons.org/licenses/by-sa/4.0>, via Wikimedia Commons: https://commons.wikimedia.org/wiki/File:Mj%C3%B8sa_2.jpg*

[26] *Bjarkan, CC BY-SA 4.0 <https://creativecommons.org/licenses/by-sa/4.0>, via Wikimedia Commons. https://commons.wikimedia.org/wiki/File:Norway_Counties_Agder_Position.svg*

[27] Bjoertvedt, CC BY-SA 3.0 <https://creativecommons.org/licenses/by-sa/3.0>, via Wikimedia Commons: https://commons.wikimedia.org/wiki/File:Panthera_tigris_kristiansand_dyrepark_IMG_4042.JPG

[28] W. Bulach, CC BY-SA 4.0 <https://creativecommons.org/licenses/by-sa/4.0>, via Wikimedia Commons: https://commons.wikimedia.org/wiki/File:.00_3198_Lindesnes_fyr_-_Museum_(Norway).jpg

[29] Basia5, CC BY 3.0 <https://creativecommons.org/licenses/by/3.0>, via Wikimedia Commons: https://commons.wikimedia.org/wiki/File:Mandal,_Norway_-_panoramio_(5).jpg

[30] Karl Ragnar Gjertsen / User:krg. This photo was taken by Karl Ragnar Gjertsen. Please credit this photo to Karl Ragnar Gjertsen in the immediate vicinity of the image. CC BY-SA 3.0 <http://creativecommons.org/licenses/by-sa/3.0/>, via Wikimedia Commons: https://commons.wikimedia.org/wiki/File:Arendal_Utsikt_02.JPG

[31] Colliekar, CC BY-SA 4.0 <https://creativecommons.org/licenses/by-sa/4.0>, via Wikimedia Commons: https://commons.wikimedia.org/wiki/File:Grimstad_078.jpg

[32] Krg, CC BY-SA 4.0 <https://creativecommons.org/licenses/by-sa/4.0>, via Wikimedia Commons: https://commons.wikimedia.org/wiki/File:TangenHis%C3%B8y.jpg

[33] Peulle, CC BY-SA 4.0 <https://creativecommons.org/licenses/by-sa/4.0>, via Wikimedia Commons: https://commons.wikimedia.org/wiki/File:Ris%C3%B8r_Krantoppen_august_2017_(2).jpg

[34] Marmelad, CC BY-SA 2.5 <https://creativecommons.org/licenses/by-sa/2.5>, via Wikimedia Commons. https://commons.wikimedia.org/wiki/File:Norway_Regions_Vestlandet_Position.svg

[35] Jerzystrzelecki, CC BY 3.0 <https://creativecommons.org/licenses/by/3.0>, via Wikimedia Commons: https://commons.wikimedia.org/wiki/File:Lysefjorden(js)01.jpg

[36] Scoundrelgeo, CC BY-SA 4.0 <https://creativecommons.org/licenses/by-sa/4.0>, via Wikimedia Commons: https://commons.wikimedia.org/wiki/File:A_man_standing_on_Kjeragbolten.jpg

[37] trolvag, CC BY-SA 3.0 <https://creativecommons.org/licenses/by-sa/3.0>, via Wikimedia Commons: https://commons.wikimedia.org/wiki/File:Stavanger_Sentrum,_Stavanger,_Rogaland,_Norway_-_panoramio.jpg

[38] TomasEE, CC BY 3.0 <https://creativecommons.org/licenses/by/3.0>, via Wikimedia Commons: https://commons.wikimedia.org/wiki/File:Sverd_i_fjell_-_panoramio_(1).jpg

[39] Florian Pépellin, CC BY-SA 3.0 <http://creativecommons.org/licenses/by-sa/3.0/>, via Wikimedia Commons: https://commons.wikimedia.org/wiki/File:Beach_of_Sola.JPG

[40] Holger Uwe Schmitt, CC BY-SA 4.0 <https://creativecommons.org/licenses/by-sa/4.0>, via Wikimedia Commons: https://commons.wikimedia.org/wiki/File:%22Bergen,_das_Herz_der_Fjorde%22_06.jpg

[41] Holger Uwe Schmitt, CC BY-SA 4.0 <https://creativecommons.org/licenses/by-sa/4.0>, via Wikimedia Commons: https://commons.wikimedia.org/wiki/File:190_Kilometer_lang_und_bis_zu_893_tief_ist_der_Hardangerfjord._03.jpg

[42] en:User:Worldtraveller,, CC BY-SA 3.0 <http://creativecommons.org/licenses/by-sa/3.0/>, via Wikimedia Commons: https://commons.wikimedia.org/wiki/File:Sognefjord,_Norway.jpg

[43] *Tomoyoshi NOGUCHI, CC BY 2.0 <https://creativecommons.org/licenses/by/2.0>, via Wikimedia Commons: https://commons.wikimedia.org/wiki/File:N%C3%A6r%C3%B8yfjord_1.jpg*

[44] *Rüdiger Stehn from Kiel, Deutschland, CC BY-SA 2.0 <https://creativecommons.org/licenses/by-sa/2.0>, via Wikimedia Commons: https://commons.wikimedia.org/wiki/File:Norwegen_1998_(209)_Jostedalsbreen_(44813773415).jpg*

[45] *Diego Delso, delso.photo, License CC-BY-SA, CC BY-SA 4.0 <https://creativecommons.org/licenses/by-sa/4.0>, via Wikimedia Commons: https://commons.wikimedia.org/wiki/File:Vista_de_%C3%85lesund_desde_Aksla,_Noruega,_2019-09-01,_DD_16.jpg*

[46] *Sundgot, CC BY-SA 4.0 <https://creativecommons.org/licenses/by-sa/4.0>, via Wikimedia Commons: https://commons.wikimedia.org/wiki/File:Geirangerfjord_1.jpg*

[47] *Edoderoo, CC BY-SA 4.0 <https://creativecommons.org/licenses/by-sa/4.0>, via Wikimedia Commons: https://commons.wikimedia.org/wiki/File:Trollstigen_(11).jpg*

[48] *https://www.pexels.com/photo/a-man-standing-at-the-peak-of-a-mountain-8724156/*

[49] *Andrei R, CC BY 3.0 <https://creativecommons.org/licenses/by/3.0>, via Wikimedia Commons: https://commons.wikimedia.org/wiki/File:Atlantic_Ocean_Road_(177685737).jpeg*

[50] *Bjarkan, CC BY-SA 4.0 <https://creativecommons.org/licenses/by-sa/4.0>, via Wikimedia Commons https://commons.wikimedia.org/wiki/File:Tr%C3%B8ndelag_2024_%E2%80%93.svg*

[51] *Holger Uwe Schmitt, CC BY-SA 4.0 <https://creativecommons.org/licenses/by-sa/4.0>, via Wikimedia Commons: https://commons.wikimedia.org/wiki/File:Die_Nidaros_Kathedrale_in_Trondheim._05.jpg*

[52] *Lars Geithe, CC BY 2.0 <https://creativecommons.org/licenses/by/2.0>, via Wikimedia Commons: https://commons.wikimedia.org/wiki/File:Smelthytta_R%C3%B8ros_(8675397842).jpg*

[53] *Sergey Ashmarin, CC BY-SA 3.0 <https://creativecommons.org/licenses/by-sa/3.0>, via Wikimedia Commons: https://commons.wikimedia.org/wiki/File:Seven_Sisters_and_The_Suitor_waterfalls_-_Geirangerfjord,_Norway_-_panoramio.jpg*

[54] *Diego Delso, CC BY-SA 4.0 <https://creativecommons.org/licenses/by-sa/4.0>, via Wikimedia Commons: https://commons.wikimedia.org/wiki/File:Islote_Munkholmen,_Trondheim,_Noruega,_2019-09-06,_DD_13.jpg*

[55] *Harald Oppedal, CC BY 3.0 <https://creativecommons.org/licenses/by/3.0>, via Wikimedia Commons: https://commons.wikimedia.org/wiki/File:Storkaia_Kristiansund.JPG*

[56] *Marmelad, CC BY-SA 2.5 <https://creativecommons.org/licenses/by-sa/2.5>, via Wikimedia Commons. https://commons.wikimedia.org/wiki/File:Norway_Regions_Nord-Norge_Position.svg*

[57] *Acediscovery, CC BY 4.0 <https://creativecommons.org/licenses/by/4.0>, via Wikimedia Commons: https://commons.wikimedia.org/wiki/File:View-Troms%C3%B8-Norway--April--2011.jpg*

[58] *Lars Palczak, CC BY-SA 4.0 <https://creativecommons.org/licenses/by-sa/4.0>, via Wikimedia Commons: https://commons.wikimedia.org/wiki/File:Alta_Church_from_Air_-_Oct_2018.jpg*

[59] *Ximonic (Simo Räsänen), CC BY-SA 3.0 <https://creativecommons.org/licenses/by-sa/3.0>, via Wikimedia Commons: https://commons.wikimedia.org/wiki/File:Oksneset_and_Ersfjorden_from_Tungeneset_in_low_sunlight,_Senja,_2012_October_-_2.jpg*

[60] *https://commons.wikimedia.org/wiki/File:Saami_Family_1900.jpg*

[61] *Eduardo Manchon, CC BY-SA 3.0 <https://creativecommons.org/licenses/by-sa/3.0>, via Wikimedia Commons: https://commons.wikimedia.org/wiki/File:North_Cape._Restaurant_Kompasset_-_panoramio.jpg*

[62] *Virtual-Pano, CC BY-SA 4.0 <https://creativecommons.org/licenses/by-sa/4.0>, via Wikimedia Commons: https://commons.wikimedia.org/wiki/File:0949_NOR_Hammerfest_polar_bear_sculpture_contre_jour_V-P.jpg*

[63] *Jorge Andrade from Rio de Janeiro, Brazil, CC BY 2.0 <https://creativecommons.org/licenses/by/2.0>, via Wikimedia Commons: https://commons.wikimedia.org/wiki/File:Lofotr_02.jpg*

[64] *Frankemann, CC BY-SA 4.0 <https://creativecommons.org/licenses/by-sa/4.0>, via Wikimedia Commons: https://commons.wikimedia.org/wiki/File:Nyholmsundet_in_the_entrance_to_Bod%C3%B8_from_north.jpg*

[65] *Harald Groven from Tromsø, Norway, CC BY-SA 2.0 <https://creativecommons.org/licenses/by-sa/2.0>, via Wikimedia Commons: https://commons.wikimedia.org/wiki/File:Rallarveien_Ofotbanen.jpg*

[66] *Arnas Goldberg, CC BY 3.0 <https://creativecommons.org/licenses/by/3.0>, via Wikimedia Commons: https://commons.wikimedia.org/wiki/File:North_Of_The_Sun_(165558753).jpeg*

[67] *https://www.pexels.com/photo/black-framed-wayfarer-style-eyeglasses-on-white-surface-917293/*

[68] *OpenStreetMap Contributors https://www.openstreetmap.org*

[69] *OpenStreetMap Contributors https://www.openstreetmap.org*

[70] *OpenStreetMap Contributors https://www.openstreetmap.org*

[71] *OpenStreetMap Contributors https://www.openstreetmap.org*

[72] *OpenStreetMap Contributors https://www.openstreetmap.org*

[73] *OpenStreetMap Contributors https://www.openstreetmap.org*

[74] *OpenStreetMap Contributors https://www.openstreetmap.org*

[75] *OpenStreetMap Contributors https://www.openstreetmap.org*

[76] *OpenStreetMap Contributors https://www.openstreetmap.org*

[77] *OpenStreetMap Contributors https://www.openstreetmap.org*

[78] *OpenStreetMap Contributors https://www.openstreetmap.org*

[79] *OpenStreetMap Contributors https://www.openstreetmap.org*

[80] *OpenStreetMap Contributors https://www.openstreetmap.org*

[81] *OpenStreetMap Contributors https://www.openstreetmap.org*

[82] *OpenStreetMap Contributors https://www.openstreetmap.org*

[83] *OpenStreetMap Contributors* https://www.openstreetmap.org
[84] *OpenStreetMap Contributors* https://www.openstreetmap.org
[85] *OpenStreetMap Contributors* https://www.openstreetmap.org
[86] *OpenStreetMap Contributors* https://www.openstreetmap.org
[87] *OpenStreetMap Contributors* https://www.openstreetmap.org

Printed in Great Britain
by Amazon

52431503R00106